The 6 St Self Mastery

Get started on a lifetime of mental clarity, physical fitness, and spiritual awareness.

Your 6 step guide to developing an Internal Power Practice.

By Derek Croley

Forward by the Author

In America today there are all kinds of things people do in the name of fitness. When I was younger I played sports- football, basketball, wrestling, track, and hard core martial art. Of course in preparation for these sports I would train in the off season with weights, running, etc.

Once my sport career was over I still continued to train with weights and even ran every now and again. To be honest, I'm not a big fan of running. My association with running is having an overweight football coach yelling, "run it again boy!" But weight training, flexibility training, calisthenics- yeah, I would do those. Of course I was training in the martial arts, that's always been my true passion.

The problem with all of this sport and sport related training is the toll it took on my body. I've done all kinds of awesome things to myself in the name of "fitness": torn out shoulder, broken ribs, at some point in time I've broken all of my fingers and toes, broken tibia, bad knees (thanks basketball), popping hips, and so on.

By the time I was in my very early twenties I couldn't lift my right arm to the side. My back always, always hurt. I couldn't turn my neck to the left. When I would sleep with my knees bent they wouldn't straighten out in the morning until I kicked my legs to pop them back in place. Good times.

This got me to thinking.

Why is all of this "fitness" stuff wrecking my body? What's going to happen to me when I'm older? At the rate I was going I would've been in a walker by 40! Not only that, I couldn't do the one thing that I really loved the most- Martial Art- at the level that I thought I should.

Fortunately, I knew the solution already- Internal Power training. I had been studying internal martial arts forms since I was a teenager (I started karate at 8) but I was only doing the forms, not the practice. For me doing Tai Chi was doing a really slow Jujitsu form without a partner. The real problem was that I knew that Tai Chi was supposed to be effortless, but I completely lacked the resources to acquire the information necessary to make it work for real. Even today it is a challenge to find Tai Chi and Qigong teachers in America that are not just dancers. Many and probably even most of them do the form but have no understanding whatsoever of what the internal power should be.

So when I was 23 I moved to China. This was not an out of the blue decision; it was something that I had known I was going to do since I was about 13. Sometimes you just have a knowing. All of the above just gave me one more reason.

I would like to say that I accepted what China had to teach me with open arms, but that would not exactly be true. I found a teacher named Liu Chan Shan. He was very gifted and taught me his form of Tai Chi as well as the art of Yuan Gong Chan Chuan, which is to this day my favorite martial art. The parts I had a difficult time accepting were some of the ways people practiced QiGong. As a very physical person it seemed silly to me as I watched people stand in the middle of a park and just bounce without jumping. Seeing people walking on a track backwards looked goofy as well.

Even though Shifu Liu tried to teach me about internal power, chi, and so on I was not a very good student. But he did plant many seeds for me to consider later on. As I have matured I have come to realize the value and intelligence of what he was trying to say as well as what the people in the park were trying to do.

For this understanding I can thank my current teacher, Xu Guo Ming. In America he goes by George Xu. Look him up on Youtube.com. George helped me put it all together, and I still have much to learn. I am thankful for this as I enjoy learning!

With this understanding I have come to realize a very simple yet important fact. ***Fitness training should make you more healthy, not more broken. Your training should mean that you will be fit now and fit when you are 80.***

This is really brought home to me as I watch the older generations of my family pass away. They are living to be plenty old enough, but in some cases they're minds go, sometimes their bodies become too broken from poor fitness, nutrition, and health habits. I see older people come in my door to take Tai Chi lessons because they have trained their bodies "conventionally" to the point that they don't work anymore.

Then I see the Chinese Internal Power Masters. Of course they get old and die eventually, but on numerous occasions I've had my butt whipped in sparring matches with 70 and 80 year old men. With most of these masters it's really hard to tell how old they are because they're skin quality is so good.

I know what you're thinking- they are a different nationality so of course I'm not good at telling their age. I might agree with this, except that I noticed this at a time that I was immersed in the culture and saw Chinese people all of the time. I was able to make direct cross comparisons.

Most importantly, when these masters get old and are on their death bed, they're minds still work. This is a big deal to me.

Something pretty cool is that these masters are in many cases willing to share information and training secrets with us. The problem, and it is a big problem, is language translation and cultural translation. It is actually pretty easy to get somebody in China who speaks English. It is really, really difficult to translate the different life perspective and philosophy from an Eastern culture to a Western culture. Most of the reason Westerners tend to dismiss Eastern ideas as airy fairy is a matter of translation of ideas and perspectives. This makes it kinda difficult to get the teachings. Not impossible, you just have to change the way you think about things a little bit. And to be honest, that is always a good thing.

With all of this said, here is what I have to offer you. This book has the beginning of the internal power information that I have learned from years of training with Chinese masters in China and in America combined with years of training and teaching the information professionally.

I have tried very hard to present this information in a way that a western mind can relate to and understand. I'm afraid you will have to deal with my sense of humor. Of course I still encourage you to train with masters if you can. Maybe this book as a base will help.

Read on to learn powerful key practices to incredible fitness and wellbeing now, and perhaps even more important, later!

Derek Croley

May 5, 2013

The 6 Steps to Self Mastery

By Derek Croley

Table of Contents

Make a choice!... 9

How to practice..33

Step 1: Align your body..45

Step 2: Wake up your spine..65

Step 3: Work the Core Agilities..88

Step 4: Work with the Earth...118

Step 5: Heaven and Earth Circulation..................................126

Step 6: Finding your Chi Body..140

The Daily Workout..169

Reference Guide...220

Copyright 2013 by Derek Croley

All rights reserved.

Sections of this book can be quoted so long as this book is credited.

ISBN-13: 978-1489522221

ISBN-10: 1489522220

Make a choice!

1. Take the Challenge!

Welcome **to The 6 Steps to Self Mastery**! By starting this program you have opened the door to better health, increased energy, stress reduction, and joy in life!

This guidebook gives you step by step, detailed information on how to make internal power training and chi body training a part of your life. This information was considered the high level secret sauce of the Tai Chi and Internal Power Masters for generations, and most of them still won't teach it to a "round eye." But herein lies the keys to a better life for you!

Learn to awaken your inner power, the energy that is already inside of you, and make it stronger! Not only that, you will learn how to use the energy that permeates the environment, how to use earth and gravity to your advantage, and how to develop what the ancient masters called the state of "natural awareness."

Just follow these six mindful steps to a healthy body, an agile mind, and spiritual balance. The total package!

> *Step 1: Align your body.*
>
> *Step 2: Activate your spine.*
>
> *Step 3: Build Core agility.*
>
> *Step 4: Play the Earth.*
>
> *Step 5: Heaven and Earth Power.*
>
> *Step 6: Find your Chi Body.*

Make up your mind. Add this practice into your mental and physical fitness regime. If you don't have one then these low impact, high result exercises are the best place to begin no matter what kind of shape you're in.

2. Why should you do this?

People have lots of reasons for taking up internal power training. Some people want to overcome an injury or an illness, some people use it to recover from a surgery, others use this kind of training to treat various medical conditions. Most are just interested in overall health and fitness for its own sake. Others still want to have more power for Martial Arts or for a sport. Some even seek spiritual growth.

What it really boils down to is anybody who has an interest in maximizing their body's efficiency, maximizing their energy flow, and harmonizing their mind, body, and spirit into a completely relaxed yet focused and alive state will gain tremendously from this kind of training.

Here is an excerpt from an article that discusses internal power training and some of its many benefits. This particular article focuses on the specific internal power art of Tai Chi, but the book you are reading is not limited to this single art.

I theorize that the Harvard people who wrote this needed the buzz word. You can find the complete

article at
http://www.health.harvard.edu/newsletters/Harvard_Womens_Health_Watch/2009/May/The-health-benefits-of-tai-chi.

No pain, big gains

Although tai chi is slow and gentle and doesn't leave you breathless, it addresses the key components of fitness — muscle strength, flexibility, balance, and, to a lesser degree, aerobic conditioning. Here's some of the evidence:

Muscle strength. *In a 2006 study published in Alternative Therapies in Health and Medicine, Stanford University researchers reported benefits of tai chi in 39 women and men, average age 66, with below-average fitness and at least one cardiovascular risk factor. After taking 36 tai chi classes in 12 weeks, they showed improvement in both lower-body strength (measured by the number of times they could rise from a chair in 30 seconds) and upper-body strength (measured by their ability to do arm curls).*

In a Japanese study using the same strength measures, 113 older adults were assigned to different 12-week exercise programs, including tai chi, brisk walking, and resistance training. People who did tai chi improved more than 30% in lower-body strength and 25% in arm strength — almost as much as those who participated in resistance training, and more than those assigned to brisk walking.

"Although you aren't working with weights or resistance bands, the unsupported arm exercise involved in tai chi strengthens your upper body," says internist Dr. Gloria Yeh, an assistant professor at Harvard Medical School. "Tai chi strengthens both the lower and upper extremities and also the core muscles of the back and abdomen."

Flexibility. *Women in the 2006 Stanford study significantly boosted upper- and lower-body flexibility as well as strength.*

Balance. *Tai chi improves balance and, according to some studies, reduces falls. Proprioception — the ability to sense the* position of one's body in space — declines with age. Tai chi helps train this sense, which is a function of sensory neurons in the inner ear and stretch receptors in the muscles and ligaments. Tai chi also improves muscle strength and flexibility, which makes it easier to recover from a stumble. Fear of falling can make you more likely to fall; some studies have found that tai chi training helps reduce that fear.

Aerobic conditioning. Depending on the speed and size of the movements, tai chi can provide some aerobic benefits. But in the Japanese study, only participants assigned to brisk walking gained much aerobic fitness. If your clinician advises a more intense cardio workout with a higher heart rate than tai chi can offer, you may need something more aerobic as well.

Selected resources

*Tai Chi Health*www.taichihealth.com

*Tai Chi Productions*www.taichiforhealth.com

*Tree of Life Tai Chi Center*www.treeoflifetaichi.com

Tai chi for medical conditions

When combined with standard treatment, tai chi appears to be helpful for several medical conditions. For example:

Arthritis. In a 40-person study at Tufts University, presented in October 2008 at a meeting of the American College of Rheumatology, an hour of tai chi twice a week for 12 weeks reduced pain and improved mood and physical functioning more than standard stretching exercises in people with severe knee osteoarthritis. According to a Korean study published in December 2008 in Evidence-based Complementary and Alternative Medicine, eight weeks of tai chi classes followed by eight weeks of home practice significantly improved flexibility and slowed the disease process in patients with ankylosing spondylitis, a painful and debilitating inflammatory form of arthritis that affects the spine.

Low bone density. A review of six controlled studies by Dr. Wayne and other Harvard researchers indicates that tai chi may be a safe and effective way to maintain bone density in postmenopausal women. A controlled study of tai chi in women with osteopenia (diminished bone density not as severe as osteoporosis) is under way at the Osher Research Center and Boston's Beth Israel Deaconess Medical Center.

Breast cancer. Tai chi has shown potential for improving quality of life and functional capacity (the physical ability to carry out normal daily activities, such as work or exercise) in women suffering from breast cancer or the side effects of breast cancer treatment. For example, a 2008 study at the University of Rochester, published in Medicine and Sport Science, found that quality of life and functional capacity (including aerobic capacity, muscular strength, and flexibility) improved in women with breast cancer who did 12 weeks of tai chi, while declining in a control group that received only supportive therapy.

Heart disease. A 53-person study at National Taiwan University found that a year of tai chi significantly boosted exercise capacity, lowered blood pressure, and improved levels of cholesterol, triglycerides, insulin, and C-reactive protein in people at high risk for heart disease. The study, which was published in the September 2008 Journal of Alternative and Complementary Medicine, found no improvement in a control group that did not practice tai chi.

Heart failure. In a 30-person pilot study at Harvard Medical School, 12 weeks of tai chi improved participants' ability to walk and quality of life. It also reduced blood levels of B-type natriuretic protein, an indicator of heart failure. A 150-patient controlled trial is under way.

Hypertension. In a review of 26 studies in English or Chinese published in Preventive Cardiology (Spring 2008), Dr. Yeh reported that in 85% of trials, tai chi lowered blood pressure — with improvements ranging from 3 to 32 mm Hg in systolic pressure and from 2 to 18 mm Hg in diastolic pressure.

Parkinson's disease. A 33-person pilot study from Washington University School of Medicine in St. Louis, published in Gait and

Posture (October 2008), found that people with mild to moderately severe Parkinson's disease showed improved balance, walking ability, and overall well-being after 20 tai chi sessions.

Sleep problems. In a University of California, Los Angeles, study of 112 healthy older adults with moderate sleep complaints, 16 weeks of tai chi improved the quality and duration of sleep significantly more than standard sleep education. The study was published in the July 2008 issue of the journal Sleep.

Stroke. In 136 patients who'd had a stroke at least six months earlier, 12 weeks of tai chi improved standing balance more than a general exercise program that entailed breathing, stretching, and mobilizing muscles and joints involved in sitting and walking. Findings were published in the January 2009 issue of Neurorehabilitation and Neural Repair.

Lots of good stuff! Let's get cracking!

a. Health, fitness, and sanity.

Do you ever feel stressed out? Tense? Scattered, like you're trying to be 20 places at once? Yeah, most people do. Internal power training can help. Here's how.

> **Tai Chi and Qi Gong Show Some Beneficial Health Effects**
>
> http://nccam.nih.gov/research/results/spotlight/071910.htm
>
> A review of scientific literature suggests that there is strong evidence of beneficial health effects of tai chi and qi gong, including for bone health, cardiopulmonary fitness, balance, and quality of life. Both tai chi and qi gong (also known as qigong) have origins in China and involve physical movement, mental focus, and deep breathing.
>
> The reviewers concluded that the evidence is sufficient to suggest that tai chi and qi gong are a viable alternative to conventional forms of exercise. They also noted that because of the similarities in philosophy and critical elements between tai chi and qi gong, the outcomes can be analyzed across both types of studies.

First, you will correct your posture. Bad posture leads to misalignment, which leads to incorrect wear and tear on your body. It also misshapes your organs, making them less efficient.

Second, you will learn to relax, even while standing. Without getting all scientific, being relaxed with correct posture allows your nervous system, circulatory system, and all of the other systems to move and flow smoothly and unhindered. Imagine taking the kinks out of a garden hose. When your body runs more smoothly and efficiently your health improves immeasurably!

Third, we will build core agility. Not only do we want your core to be strong, we also want it to be agile and intelligent. This helps make sure that all of your organs are functioning at their peak, gives you an incredibly better center of balance, and decreases your chances of hurting yourself with poor body mechanics.

Here's a little something from our friends at Harvard. http://www.health.harvard.edu/healthbeat/the-real-world-benefits-of-strengthening-your-core.

The real-world benefits of strengthening your core

Think of your core muscles as the sturdy central link in a chain connecting your upper and lower body. Whether you're hitting a tennis ball or mopping the floor, the necessary motions either originate in your core, or move through it.

No matter where motion starts, it ripples upward and downward to adjoining links of the chain. Thus, weak or inflexible core muscles can impair how well your arms and legs function. And that saps power from many of the moves you make. Properly building up your core cranks up the power. A strong core also enhances balance and stability. Thus, it can help prevent falls and injuries during sports or other activities. In fact, a strong, flexible core underpins almost everything you do:

- **Everyday acts.** Bending to put on shoes or scoop up a package, turning to look behind you, sitting in a chair, or simply standing still — these are just a few of the many mundane actions that rely on your core and that you might not notice until they become difficult or painful. Even basic activities of daily living — bathing or dressing, for example — call on your core.
- **On-the-job tasks.** Jobs that involve lifting, twisting, and standing all rely on core muscles. But less obvious tasks — like sitting at your desk for hours — engage your core as well. Phone calls, typing, computer use, and similar work can make back muscles surprisingly stiff and sore, particularly if you're not strong enough to practice good posture and aren't taking sufficient breaks.
- **A healthy back.** Low back pain — a debilitating, sometimes excruciating problem affecting four out of five Americans at some point in their lives — may be prevented by exercises that promote well-balanced, resilient core muscles. When back pain strikes, a regimen of core exercises is often prescribed to relieve it, coupled with medications, physical therapy, or other treatments if necessary.

- **Sports and other pleasurable activities.** Golfing, tennis or other racquet sports, biking, running, swimming, baseball, volleyball, kayaking, rowing and many other athletic activities are powered by a strong core. Less often mentioned are sexual activities, which call for core power and flexibility, too.
- **Housework, fix-it work, and gardening.** Bending, lifting, twisting, carrying, hammering, reaching overhead — even vacuuming, mopping, and dusting are acts that spring from, or pass through, the core.
- **Balance and stability.** Your core stabilizes your body, allowing you to move in any direction, even on the bumpiest terrain, or stand in one spot without losing your balance. Viewed this way, core exercises can lessen your risk of falling.
- **Good posture.** Weak core muscles contribute to slouching. Good posture trims your silhouette and projects confidence. More importantly, it lessens wear and tear on the spine and allows you to breathe deeply. Good posture helps you gain full benefits from the effort you put into exercising, too.

Weak, tight, or unbalanced core muscles can undermine you in any of these realms. And while it's important to build a strong core, it's unwise to aim all your efforts at developing rippling abs. Overtraining abdominal muscles while snubbing muscles of the back and hip can set you up for injuries and cut athletic prowess. If washboard abs are your holy grail, it's essential to trim body fat through diet and aerobic exercise and build strong abdominal muscles through frequent core exercise sessions.

Forth, we will find your chi body. By relaxing your physical body and moving your mind energy around, you will be mentally sharper, more balanced emotionally, and generally more in tune with life, the universe and everything. Whatever your daily stresses are, this will keep you sane my friend!

b. Martial Arts mega ninja powers.

This kind of information is generally taught in martial arts after the student has mastered all of the techniques, or has reached a certain age and maturity. The reason that a martial artist or an athlete would want to learn this stuff is pretty simple: tremendous power.

Even the power to defeat the Joker. Well, after he's put on a few pounds.

These internal power practices are kind of like replacing the copper top battery you've been running off of with a nuclear reactor. It will offer you huge amounts of practically unlimited power.

So much so that you become well-nigh undefeatable and no longer even need techniques to thwart evil.

So… you know… you've got that goin' for ya.

With the man I earned my first Black Belt from, Kyoshi Dave Kovar. He is a true inspiration to everybody he meets. I am Batman.

c. Spiritual development.

The key to spiritual development is the harmonization with your body, chi, and mind, and then harmonizing that with your environment. Reaching higher levels of self is about nothing more than refinement. Those on a spiritual path use internal power training to first, distinguish the physical from the chi, and then the chi from the mind. Then they learn how to harmonize 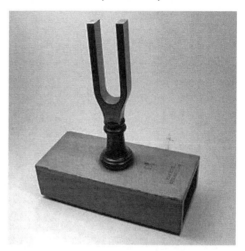 these components. Remember, the mind leads the chi, and the chi leads the body. These things must be balanced like a highly refined scale, and harmonized like a tuning fork.

However, you must be able to retain this refined harmony in relation to the outside world, your environment. Do not hide from the world as some forms of meditation would have you do, rather be in balance with it.

In the end this refinement of self leads you to simply see what is there. Not what you were told should be there, not what you want to be there, not what you think should be there- just what actually is.

Internal power training is the best way to do this.

With my teacher Grand Master George Xu. Though I have studied under numerous teachers and learned a lot from all of them, George is the person who was able to help me really grasp high level internal power and martial arts. One of the really inspiring things about him is that even in his 60's he is better, more refined, every time I see him. There is a lesson there.

2. The quest for immortality...or at least still being you when you're all old and crunchy.

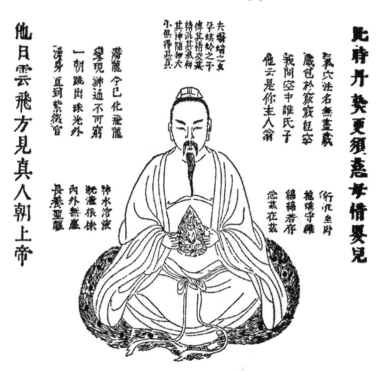

An old immortal dude. Thanks Wiki!

Chi body and internal power training are often likened to becoming an immortal. This doesn't seem to hold true since the masters keep on getting old and dying, but if you think about it, it does make sense historically.

People used to not live all that long. Peasants would be worked to the bone and die in their twenties. Royalty would live lavishly and die in their thirties. Internal power masters would live into their seventies. For such a time period living three generations would sure seem like immortality.

These days living to be 80 or 90 is not uncommon, in fact we think something has gone wrong if we don't. The thing is, what will your mental and physical condition be with you get to be that old? The biggest benefit that I've seen is that even though the internal power masters do die at the normal modern ages, they tend to have their full mental facilities and their bodies tend to be in excellent condition for their relative ages. Being 80 and having the skin of a 40 year old doesn't sound that bad….

3. Getting Started!

First off, keep in mind that this is really a reference guide. You do really need to train under a qualified instructor like, well, me. You can read this and understand it, but to really get it right you need to have  somebody teaching you to read your body quality. This can be done in weekly classes or workshops and seminars. Classes are better, but weekend events are better than nothing!

However, should this stop you from getting started if you haven't taken a class or seminar yet?

NOOOOOO!!!!! All you need to get started is enough space to stand up in. Well, actually, not even that. You can do this stuff sitting or lying down as well. So really, to get started all you have to do is GET STARTED! Anything else is just a lame excuse.

And **why be lame when you can be awesome?**

Me punching a Karate dude. Because I am awesome and can totally do stuff like that.

4. Finding the Time….

People tend to be creatures of habit. So make internal power training a habit. First, set aside 10-15 minutes every morning to go through the practice you will find at the end of this book.

Wait, what? You have an excuse not to? Let's talk about that for a second. When you don't want to train or don't have time to train is when you especially need to be training! As soon as you stop sharpening your saw it starts to get dull. When it's hardest to train you need to actively change your thinking.

Change "I'm tired" to *"When I finish I'll feel energized."*

Change "I'm way too busy. There's too much going on" to *"Once I've finished some internal power training I'll be thinking clearer and be better able to prioritize and organize."*

Change "I'll do it tomorrow" to *"Why wait to feel great!"*

The thing that most people miss is that this relaxation, stress management, and personal balance and harmony stuff is not something that you practice for 10 minutes in the morning and then forget about.

Do this stuff all of the time! Always be training correct body, correct balance, and correct mind.

Driving your car? Great, work internal power.

Boss yelling at you? Great, work on sending that negative energy into the floor with internal power.

Did the kids do whatever thoughtless or gross thing kids do? Awesome, work on relaxing and calming down with internal power.

And so on and so forth....

The idea is simple. Make internal power, mental intent, and chi body just how you exist. Stress will just poor off of you like water on a duck- not from ignoring it, rather from being relaxed in the moment. This means that you will be so much more balanced and better able to deal with whatever is happening without going nuts!

5. **Make Internal Power training part of your overall fitness program.**

Maybe you already have an awesome training system that works great for you, but it just needs a few simple adjustments. Maybe you work a lot and just don't have time to work out. Maybe you are not happy with your body right now, for whatever reason, and want to improve it, but don't know where to start.

One quick thought. If you already have a physical training regime, make sure that it is actually designed for your health, fitness, well-being, and longevity. Do not do things that will destroy your body later with the notion that you are getting in shape now. Breaking yourself is not the same thing as health and fitness.

This is not an excuse to do nothing, just use your brain.

In all cases, right where you are is the perfect place to begin. Who you are right now is the reality of who you are. This is not only okay, this is awesome! You are in the perfect position to access your internal power, find your chi body, and harmonize your body, mind, and spirit.

Let's get started!

How to Practice.

1. Relax buddy- it's quality, not quantity!

Don't set time limits for yourself. Instead of measuring time spent on a daily practice session measure your level of relaxation and focus.

This dude needs to relax.

Remember that we are after a sensation, not racing a clock.

Also, for each exercise, it doesn't matter how many repetitions you do. Don't even count them. Just do each exercise until you are finished with it and want to go on to the next. Relax buddy, just chill.

Oh, and sometimes you will hear that you must do this kind of training at a certain time of day, facing a certain direction, and other specific rules. Disregard this stuff. It really doesn't matter. It is referring to the idea that electromagnetic currents go through the earth, ie, the Van Allen Radiation Belt.

This is a real thing, but we are training your chi body in a three dimensional manner, so it doesn't really matter which part of you is facing where, just like it doesn't matter which part of a basketball you dribble with.

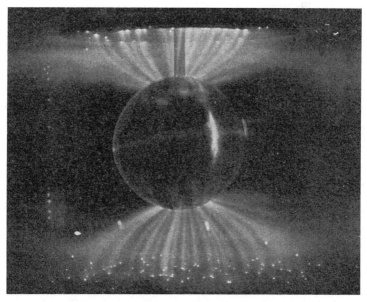

A lab simulation of the Van Allen belt according to Wikipedia.

2. Calm down, don't be so hard on yourself.

I took this picture walking just outside of the city in Dali, China. We originally planned on staying there for only a couple of days, but liked it so much we stayed for two weeks.

Most adults have the expectation that they should be able to be good at anything they try quickly if not immediately. We are adults after all, right? Many of my students have at some point in time forgotten what it is like to be a student who doesn't have all of the answers.

I can't tell you how many students I've had who have trained in this material for three months and then declared, "I'm just not getting this right! I understand that mastering the chi body took years for all of the masters, but I'm me! I should be able to do it immediately!" Or some other such stupidity.

Remember, this is a path. It is not a sprint, it is not a marathon. There is no finish line. This is more like a pleasant walk through the woods where you constantly get to discover cool new things.

Seek enjoyment and pleasure in steady personal refinement. The great thing about this is that you will be better at internal power when you are 90 than when you are 30. The only way to fail is to stop training.

Sometimes it's good to act like a kid!

3. Stuff you need to get started.

You don't need much. In fact, you don't need anything except your mind and body. However, here is a list of some things that you might find useful in helping you set the right mood for yourself.

- Comfy, flat soled shoes.
- Loose fitting workout clothes. (Having an outfit that you train in helps get your mind in the right place.)
- Outside is nice. (You can train anywhere, but being outside is always good if you have some nature type stuff to look at.)
- This book. (At least until you have the routine memorized.)

4. Where can you train?

Like I said, outside is nice, but anywhere is just fine. You can train in your bed room, your living room, your back porch, your front porch, your yard, in your car, in your office, standing in line at the grocery store, walking around the mall, out in the woods on a hike....

You get the idea- absolutely anywhere! Oh, and if you're out in public waving your arms around and somebody asks you what you are doing, tell them about this book. Well, unless you're being run off or arrested. Then don't mention it or me.

Me on the Great Wall of China. I always get a kick out of people doing kung fu poses and training montages up here. I should've. Next time I guess.

5. Safety Frog to the rescue!

One of the great things about internal power training is that it is a very low impact training system and as such it is very, very difficult to hurt yourself. In fact, I've never heard of anybody hurting themselves doing this kind of thing.

Well, some people do crazy things in the name of chi practices that anybody with an ounce of common sense knows is a bad idea. For example, don't go around tying weights to your privates (yeah, who knew, right?) or any other things that are, uhm, just plain dangerously weird. And I'm not kidding, that is a real thing.

However, if you do have any physical limitations, injuries, or whatever it is no problem at all to modify internal power training however you need to for your own safety. Most of my students are over the age of 25, and therefore have some kind of injury. It is no problem at all to work around whatever your issues are and modify things as needed.

6. The Daily format.

When I say that you can train anywhere any time, I mostly mean that you can do the internal exercises without waving your arms around while standing or sitting in place. Nobody will be able to see what you are doing and you can practice to your heart's content.

I do all of the time. In fact, as I sit here writing I am doing internal power exercises.

With the morning routine where you do wave your arms around, it will go something like this:

Part 1: Physical Alignment and power stretches.

Part 2: Core agility and internal power exercises.

Part 3: Chi and mental focus training exercises.

This will be listed in detail later, once we have gone over a little more information, but this will hopefully give you an idea of a general format as we get started.

7. Make it part of your life!

This isn't the kind of thing that you can do for 10 minutes in the morning and then you're good for the rest of the day. That's a good start, but stress happens all of the time, not only for a few minutes in the morning. That's why you have to make using internal power just who and what you are.

On the other hand, one of the great things about practicing internal power is that you can do it all of the time! You can use these skills during stressful situations to just dump the stress right then. You can practice using the greater efficiency and power while you are doing anything you might generally do over the course of your day.

Try to drive your car with internal power.
Try to open doors with internal power.
Try to use a fork and knife with internal power.
Try to sit with internal power.
Try to walk with internal power.
Get the idea?

Don't make internal power training something that you do for a while in the morning and then just forget about. Make these qualities and principles what you are! Make this how you use and think about your body. Make internal power an actual part of your life!

Now let's get to work on specifically what you should be doing!

Step 1: Align Your Body.

The very first thing you need is to correct your posture. All kinds of physical problems come from having bad posture.

- ➤ **Bad posture** makes your joints wear incorrectly- leading to bad knees, ankles, hips, shoulders….
- ➤ **Bad posture** makes your organs all squelched up wrong- leading to all kinds of kinks and clogs.
- ➤ **Bad posture** makes your blood circulation more difficult- leading to whatever problems arise from poor blood flow.
- ➤ **Bad posture** kinks up your nervous system- making your body not communicate with itself very well.
- ➤ **Bad posture** is bad for your back- I can't tell you how many people I meet who have no idea why they experience back pain….
- ➤ **Bad posture** leads to neck pain- so get your head on straight, you goon.

- **Bad posture** makes your muscles clench up to do your skeletons job- making you store that stress you seem to eat like candy.
- **Bad posture** makes you look lame, which is the opposite of cool or awesome. Once again, why be lame when you can be awesome? Be more like a ninja.

- ✓ **Good posture** allows you to use your joints correctly- meaning they stay healthy longer.
- ✓ **Good posture** makes your organs sit correctly in your body- meaning they function more efficiently.
- ✓ **Good posture** makes your circulatory system flow unhindered- making every cell in your body more efficient.
- ✓ **Good posture** unkinks your nervous system- creating optimal communication from one part of your body to the next.
- ✓ **Good posture** fixes a lot of back pain issues- you may have screwed it up too much to fix it entirely, but taking stress off of your back and putting it on the floor is a good way to go.

- ✓ **Good posture** takes stress off of your neck- all of that tension can now melt away to the ground.
- ✓ **Good posture** allows your muscles to melt into a relaxed state- which is better for releasing stress and tension, and allows your body's internal power to do its thing without you getting in the way.
- ✓ **Good posture** makes you look awesome. Ninjas, Pirates and Chewbacca all have good posture. I rest my case.

Good posture fixes a lot of problems. The basic idea is pretty simple: your skeleton is made to hold

your body up and your muscles are made to move it. When your muscles are doing your skeleton's job there are problems. Furthermore, when you align your skeletal structure it doesn't wear and tear incorrectly. Your muscles will be relaxed, your joints will be in good shape, and all of your juices will be flowing optimally.

I'm going to go into some more detail here in a moment, but there is a general principle to follow here.

Stand sideways in front of a mirror. Lift your head straight up, then make sure that your temple, the ball of the shoulder joint, the ball of the hip joint, and the middle of your foot line up.

That's a pretty important thing to get right. Most people keep their hips too far forward, their back to slouched, their shoulders up, forward, and broken, and their head hanging forward.

A fun game to play is to look at people's body quality wherever you go. Look for broken shoulders, broken posture, hanging heads, stuff like that. Good fun.

But enough of that, let's look at some more details of what you should be doing for correct alignment. Here's what you do.

Training in Langfang, China with Grand Master Wu Ji. He had very high level Spirit Power. To find out what that is just keep reading.

1. **Head up.**

Lift your head up. Most people make the mistake of lifting their chin, which is of course completely and utterly wrong. Instead, lift the back of your head, with your chin slightly down.

Now line up your temple with the ball of your shoulder and the ball of your hip. For most people, this means to have your head sit back a bit from its normal position.

The relevant points on the head are

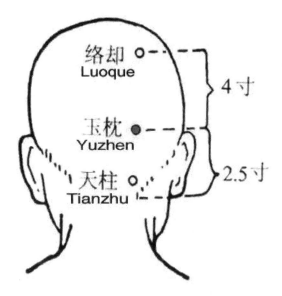

The Yu Zhen, or "*Jade Pillow*," which is the little bone sticking out at the very top of the spine at the bottom of the skull. This point needs to have an upward lift to it. Do not confuse up with out, they are not the same thing. Go with up. This will brighten your eyes, help with headaches, and help with vertigo. I've had several students train with me solely to correct vertigo, and they tell me that they get really good results.

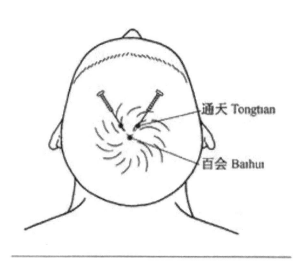

Fig. 4-5 Tongtian-pointing-to-Hui needling

The Baihui, or "**Point of 100 Crossings**," is at the top of your head. Lift this straight up as if a parachute is attached to it, lifting you. This by the way, I'm told will take away anxiety and help a great deal with depression.

2. Shoulders back.

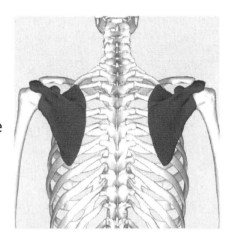

One of the key things to get right is your shoulder position. Most people do not have this right. If your shoulders are not attached to your torso, then they will operate by themselves without the power of

The Shoulder Joint

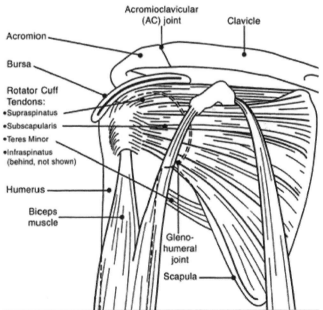

the rest of your body. The basic idea is that you want your shoulders to ride on top of, and be a part of, your body. We like to call this concept "back up body mass," or "unit force." Meaning to use the body to back up what you are doing with your arms.

So here's what you do to get correct shoulder structure. Hold your shoulders down. Then, push your shoulders back so there is no fold between your chest and shoulder in the front of your body. Next, roll your shoulder blade out to the sides and under the armpit so it does not stick out from your back. Your back should feel flat, i.e. no shoulder blade sticking out, if somebody where to run their hand across it.

Doing this is good for fixing shoulder and arm pain. When I was in middle school I separated my shoulder in a wrestling practice. Unfortunately, I missed a big chunk of the season that year. At any rate, by the time I was twenty I often couldn't lift my arm and my shoulder was constantly in pain.

When I learned how to use this method, even at this low level of internal power, my pain went away and I regained full use of my right arm again. Pretty cool if you ask me.

3. Lower back out.

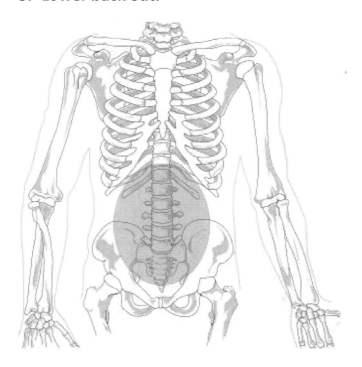

You want your back to be straight. Lift your head as previously mentioned, open your lower back out, and push your tailbone down. The back is so important that the entire next chapter is about it.

Keep your back straight but agile and alive like a predatory animal.

One of the key points to think about on the back is the Mingmen, or the **"Stone Gate."** This is the place on your lower back where the nerves in your spine branch out like a girdle into your abdomen. This is important as it is a key point for communication between your brain and your organs. A lot of tension here can mess things up.

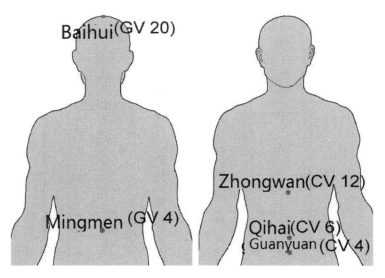

http://en.tcm-china.info/health/method/77196_7.shtml

4. Knees and hips out.

At one of the workshops I instructed several years ago, there were a lot of female runners. One of the common complaints that they had was ankle pain while running. Just by looking at the women who has this complaint it was easy to see what the problem was- their ankles were bowed in due to their hip structure. All they had to do was keep their knees in a straight line with their hips and the ankle problems would go away. It was simply an issue of alignment.

That's just an example, but a lot of people have some kind of hip, knee, or ankle pain that can be fixed merely by checking your alignment.

So here's what you do. Turn your knees just slightly out. Do it only enough to feel the ball joint in your hip have a slight sensation of opening. That's really about it. Don't overdo this- make sure it's just enough- don't over rotate.

Also, when you move, make sure that you keep your knees over your toes and your hips over your knees.

This is called opening the kua, or the V of the hips and is important for creating core movement later on. However, don't confuse skeletal structure stuff with internal power stuff nor chi stuff. We'll get that later.

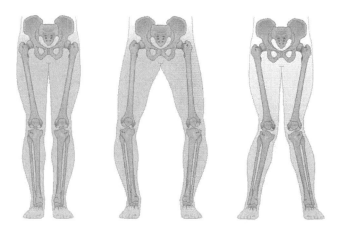

Open the V of the hip by gently opening out the knees.
Thanks again wiki for this pic.

5. Feet flat.

We eventually want your feet to become alive and to control your body's movement, but for the time being let's just work on structure, especially since we are in the structure chapter still. So here goes.

When your hips, knees, and ankles are lined up, your feet will be pretty well flat on the ground as they should be. That's really about it.

Sometimes you will hear people talk about equalizing the four corners of the foot to make sure they are flat. This is a pretty good beginning

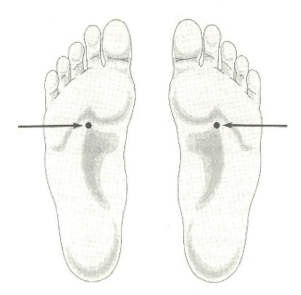

exercise if your hips are opened and the entire leg alignment has been addressed. Otherwise this is beginning in the wrong place and you're just going to trash your ankles. I don't think you'll have fun with that.

Also, keep in mind the yongquan, or "**Bubbling Well**" point at the middle bottom of your foot. This is your physical connection to earth chi and when it's messed up you tend to feel light headed, might vomit, and may feel constipated. Hey, that sounds like fun doesn't it?

This earth chi connection is a pretty important point to remember later on when we discuss earth power.

In conclusion to the skeletal structure and alignment section, just keep your posture in mind. It's important. To summarize and review:

- Lift the back of the head, chin a little down.
- Shoulders down. Blades back, under, and flat. No fold in the front nor the back of the shoulders.
- Back flat.
- Hips open, knees gently rotated out.
- Hips, knees, and feet lined up.

Build the habit of having good alignment, then over time work on melting the muscle around it. The end result of this level should be that you feel relaxed.

If someone were to touch you when you are at this level they should feel like all of your power is coming from your skeleton and tendons- not from your muscles.

Step 2: Wake Up Your Spine.

You probably didn't know this, but your spine is kind of important. As my sister in law would say, "I know, right?"

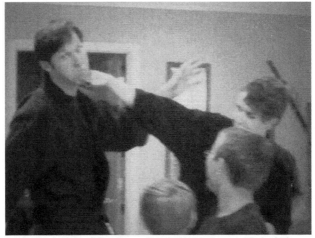

Sometimes you get hit. I usually get hit inadvertently by kids.

I've been told that sometimes fighters who carry their spine incorrectly can damage their pericardium, the sheath around the heart, by doing heavy bag work. It seems that the force that bounces back into the body can reverberate back down that spine, bounce off the incorrect top of the lumbar curve, and mess up the heart. Interesting idea. I've never bothered to fact check this (might mess up a fun story with a pesky reality), but it reads good.

The spine is the beginning of the **Zhong Ding** line, or center equilibrium. More on this later.

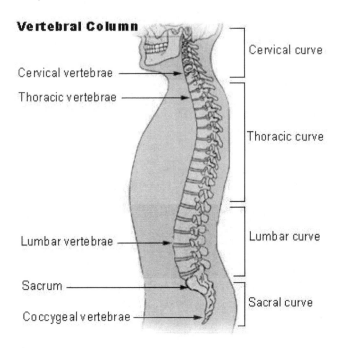

It has been said that there are three barriers along the spine. These are barriers to the chi flow up the back. They are the afore mentioned **Jade Pillow** at the base of the skull. Next is the lulu, or "**The Pully,**" which is at the top of the lumbar curve, sort of in the middle of the back. And finally is the weilü, or "**the Caudal Funnel**." This one is at the bottom of the spine.

But who cares, that's just me trying to sound all fancy. I don't even speak Chinese and I live in America- making speaking in Chinese kind of useless. To be honest, I've always found it rather silly and contrived when people speak in a foreign language that they don't really speak just so they can sound important. Ironically this makes me say things in Chinese sometimes just to make fun of this very phenomenon. And any time you hear me talking about "energy" I'm probably being snarky as well.

Anyway, what really matters is much simpler. Get the top, middle, and bottom of the spine to straighten and open up. That's pretty much it. Let's talk about how to do that.

1. Forget step 1, just melt.

Yes, you read that correctly. Once you have step one, physical alignment, forget it. Consider it a good stretch to do daily, but there is an interesting thing about internal power training. Once you have one level down fairly well, destroy it. What was once liberating becomes a prison if you do not rise above it.

There is no "it." There is no destination. There is only never ending improvement. Do not view your training as a sprint. Do not even view it as a marathon. Rather, view it as a walk in the woods full of more wonders with every step. So long as you continue the walk, you continue to learn and grow. The only way to fail is to stop.

Let's talk about melting, also called **Song**. In fact, since I'm feeling lazy, here is a blog post I wrote on the subject some time ago on WhiteOakMartialArts.com.

The Power of Song

I enjoy a good tune as much as anybody, but in this case we are talking about the Chinese word "song," meaning relax. Almost everybody carries a great deal of tension around in their minds and bodies. One of the first things we do in internal martial arts is to train relaxation. First to be relaxed while still, and then to be relaxed while moving.

This is incredibly valuable on many levels. First is that this is obviously an excellent way to manage stress. People carry emotional stress in their bodies, especially in their shoulders and neck. The first thing we work on is to relax this area.

Pretty soon you will get so good at achieving "song" that you will be able to relax at will.

Second, you will find that being able to relax leads to a great deal of mental clarity. You will be able to immediately dump stress- enabling you to think more clearly under pressure. The trick of this is to relax the body and activate the mind. In Chinese martial arts they say to have a relaxed body and an alive mind. This enables your body to be empty and calm while your mind is aware and active.

Third, the ability to relax is great for self-defense. It enables you be dead weight- which is difficult to for somebody else to move, and easy for you to maximize your personal power.

So relax buddy! Melt! Melt everything into the floor. Let your tension drip away, step by step, bit by bit.

Most people have difficulty in the following areas when trying to melt.

The neck, shoulders and upper back are #1. This is where we carry tons of stress. So much so, that most people have these muscles locked up incredibly tight.

In fact, most people that I meet have had these muscles so locked up for so long that they have essentially turned to stone. I used to have this problem and have worked really hard to deal with it.

Tissue builds up, especially around the bottom of the neck that in essence just solidifies. What do you do with this? Stretch it. A lot. In the exercises section of this book we'll go over neck looseners. I also recommend massage therapy and acupuncture along with Internal Power Training to get things moving.

The next trouble spot would be the lower back. The erectus spinae (lower back muscles) are tough to loosen up. This will come with shrinking and expanding the spine and working the Mingmen (i.e., gently pushing out your lower back to make your spine straight). When I first loosened up my lower back it was so sore that I bought a new mattress. Unclenching locked up muscles will cause some soreness. Did I mention that?

And the last major tension spot to melt will be the hip flexors. They are the little muscle on the front of your hip, or what they like to call the kua in Chinese. To melt these you will have to maintain good posture (head up, hips and shoulders in line) and then kind of sit back. The trick is to keep your back relaxed and straight while at the same time keeping the front of your hips relaxed and not pushed forward. To do this you roll your hips like a wheel instead of pushing them forward or backward.

To test this yourself, see if you can fit three fingers into the fold that should have formed where your hip meets your leg. A little pocket should form there. If it hasn't, or if the hip flexor feels hard, you don't have it yet.

The whole phrase of melting comes from the three phases of water. A person who is really stiff and physical is called an "ice man." Not in the cool X-

Men kind of way, more in a "look how lame that dude is" kind of way. Next would be "water man." This person is very relaxed and flowy, but doesn't necessarily have good body unit connection and probably doesn't have good power. Finally is "steam man." Steam man is lighter than water and has pressure, therefore more power. So the idea of melting is to melt away the ice- stiffness in your body- to become water. Then let the water evaporate away to become steam.

A good way to practice melting is with breathing exercises. It's pretty simple, every time you exhale, let yourself relax a little bit more. Start at the top of your body with the relaxing bit, and then work your way down. That's all there is to at... at least at this point. It gets fancier later though. So, you know, relax. Take a load off. It gets better. Honest. Look over there.

The 6 Steps to Self Mastery. 74

AHHHHH!!! I'm meltinggggggggg......

2. Elongate the spine.

Lift your head, push your tailbone down, and let your lower back relax out.

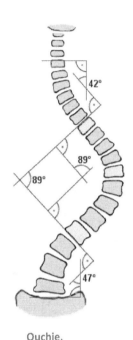

Ouchie.

Waking up the spine is incredibly good for your overall health and fitness. Your posture will get better, some people tell me they even get taller. Your nervous system will become more agile and alive. Your neck will not kink up as much. Your back pain will dramatically decrease.

I have scoliosis, as I recall in high school my back had a 22 degree curve. So of course, as I got older it would go out all of the time, practically daily, and it always hurt. It was very common for me to wake up and not be able to turn my head. Did I mention that it always hurt?

Well, as I started doing this straightening, shrinking, and expanding exercise I noticed a few things. First, my pain is gone. Second, my back very rarely goes out, and when it does I can fix it quickly. Third, my neck turns to both sides with no clicks, cracks, or grunts of pain.

So, yeah, for me this one has been a pretty big deal.

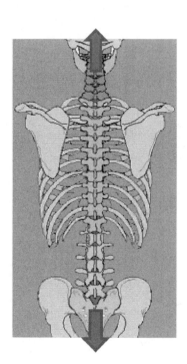

The 6 Steps to Self Mastery. 77

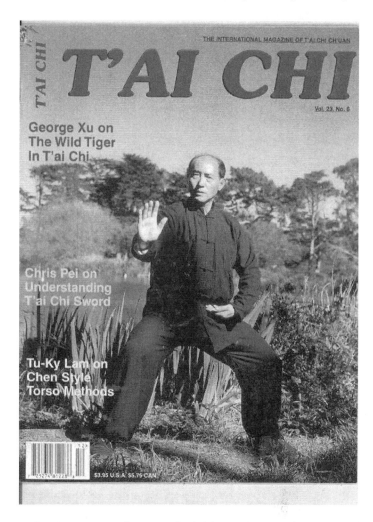

My teacher George Xu on the cover of Tai Chi Magazine. Good posture on that fellow. If you ever get the chance, I encourage you to train with him.

3. Long lever Power.

The Zhong Ding, or central equilibrium. I should have shrinking and expanding up and down power.

Here is where we will go into the idea of the Zhong Ding power I briefly mentioned earlier. No, don't bother looking back, I didn't say anything all that important. In fact, here is all it said, "The spine is the beginning of the Zhong Ding line, or center equilibrium. More on this later."

Here's the later.

By lifting your head in the prescribed manner, and then doing all of this other stuff with your spine we've been discussing, you can continue the line down to your center of balance between your feet.

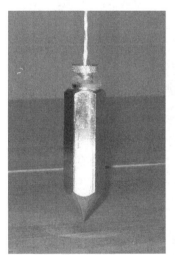
I am a plumb bob.

Imagine tying a plumb bob to the top of your head that can hang straight down through your body. Where the weight dangles on the floor is where your center of balance is.

When you use your back as I'm telling you to and keep this plumb bob idea in mind you will discover your Central Equilibrium, or Zhong Ding.

You can use this understanding of a correct spine along with knowing your center of balance on the floor to create a lever from the ground with which you can create total body leverage.

Enter the long lever concept. This is also called maximum leverage. The idea is to use the leverage of your entire body from the floor up to generate power for whatever you are doing. Most people

generate power from their shoulders or lower back. Both are unsupported by the floor and have generally poor leverage for generating power.

Long Lever power means to use your central equilibrium from the floor up to generate power. To do this you have to have your movement come from your feet and be guided by the head, with your body melted.

A good analogy for this is a car jack. You position the jack to use leverage from the ground to lift something heavy. This is the basic idea of how you should use your body.

4. Spiraling.

Spiraling power is a pretty important thing as well. I have been told- though I've never actually bothered to do the math myself, that you can negate about 40% of incoming force with spiraling power, if you like to talk all fancy you can call it "Chan Su Jin."

One time I spent an entire private lesson with a Chinese Tai Chi Master learning about Chan Su Jin. The problem was that I had no idea that this translated to spiraling. I did gather that it had to do with using my feet. We had what you might call a communication problem as he was speaking Chinglish and Chinese and I was speaking Chinglish and redneck. It took me about a year to figure out that Chan Su Jing and Spiraling Power were one and the same. This story has no point, I just thought it would be fun to share.

So how do you do this Chan Su Spiraling Stuff Thingy? Use your feet. Pay attention to the bottom of your feet where they are in contact with the floor. Without moving them on the ground, give forward pressure to one foot and backward pressure to the other. Lo and behold, your body will turn.

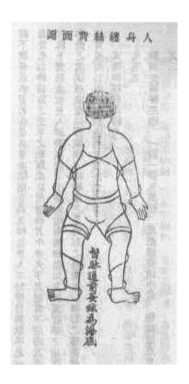

Use this secret ninja power like your hands on the steering wheel of your car. They turn the wheel just enough to create the motion in the car that you want. Same with your feet. Push and pull them on the ground to create the motion that you want.

I say this because most of the books out there talk about spiraling in a way that makes it seem like you should be spinning your legs around like Linda Blair's head.

Nah man, chill out- melt. Just push and pull your feet on the ground enough to create the spiral that you want. Then keep the rest of your body melted with your head suspended. This way you can have the spiral from your feet go up into every part of your body. All you have to do is get out of the way and let it happen. Beginning with your feet interacting with the floor, then let it continue on up your body to your hands.

Can you get the spiraling from your feet intelligent enough to make your fingers spiral?

There are levels to spiraling power. In fact there are generally three levels to everything with internal power.

For spiraling they are snake, dragon, and then tornado.

If the central equilibrium and spiraling is complete to the feet but is kind of small, it is a snake. If it is larger- as large as your entire body, then you have dragon spiraling power. If your spiraling power feels larger than your body then you have tornado power.

This is the kind of thing that a book can tell you exists, but unfortunately you will have to actually touch and do kinetic testing to really understand what I'm talking about.

This is a good time for a shameless plug. Come to one of my classes or workshops, or book me for one, and I will be happy to demonstrate and explain this to you in person.

5. Shrinking and expanding the spine.

I mentioned this earlier, but let's go into a little more detail. This is where you work your spine like a pump.

Just shrink and expand your spine like a piston, pushing the bottom down and the head up, then relaxing.

The mistake that most people make is that they think of the spine as a metal bar that doesn't move. It's better to think of it as a snake that can move, shrink, and generally be alive.

So work out the kinks, shrink and expand. Extend and relax. Work your spine and make it alive. In the last chapter of this book we will go over some exercises to help you with this. I tend to do this all of the time. I'm shrinking and expanding my spine right now as I write this. I'm sitting on an old couch at a horse farm in Florida by the way. You can do this anywhere, anytime, in any position. And you should.

Step 3: Work the Core Agilities.

Everybody is always talking about strengthening their core. This is almost a good thing. But there are, of course, some problems here. Having a strong core is good, but it is better to have an agile and intelligent core.

It's kind of like when I used to play football in school. The kid who was super strong in the weight room was never as good on the field as the kid who had intelligent strength from working on a peach farm. Yes, we were in South Carolina. Lots and lots of peaches. Intelligent and agile strength is always better and more useful than weight room strength. The weight room guy was always super strong in one single direction, but was worthless if the angle changed even a little.

The same holds true here. Your core needs to be agile and alive, able to shrink and expand and spiral. Do not train it to only clench up like a board. Make it alive like a predatory animal.

Let's use as a case study the most successful hunter in the world, aside from us talking monkeys. Yes, I mean the house cat. Tough little things.

In my back yard I have a six foot privacy fence. My family has a cat named Reepicheep (a Narnia reference and a poorly named cat. He is nothing like Reepicheep in the story). Reepicheep the cat will stand right next to the six foot fence and do a standing vertical leap to the top of the fence. I'm much taller than he is and I can't do a standing vertical leap to the top of the fence.

I know cats have a different skeleton than we do thus enabling them to do stuff like this to a much greater efficiency, but the point is that we can do a heck of a lot better with core agility than most people

Lipofski Basketballphoto.com

bother to do. As a case in point I submit to you most Olympic athletes and Michael Jordan. Who I guess eventually did become an Olympic athlete. Even if we are not athletes such as Jordan we can aspire to more body agility and intelligence than we currently do. More than the untrained even consider possible.

Cats have insanely awesome core agility and intelligence. That's why kung fu guys are always going on and on and on about tigers. Tigers are a perfect example of melted power and core agility

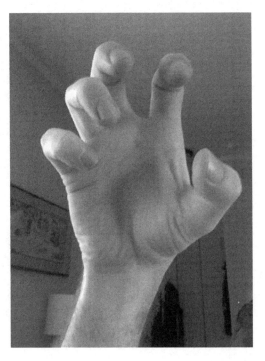

and intelligence. Between you and me, I always get a kick out of watching kung fu dudes jump around pretending to be a tiger, posing and holding their hands in like this scrunched up tiger claw fist thingy. They are totally missing the point of the tiger reference from which the kung fu style was designed. Grrrr. It isn't how you hold your hand and pose, it's how you move and use your body. It's how you perceive yourself.

Core intelligence is also said to be great for your organ function, position, and overall health. The masters say that by moving around and massaging your organs with intelligent core movement they tend to stay alive and in better health longer. They refer to this as third hand power.

The idea of third hand power is that your hands tend to stay flexible and useful longer than other parts of the body because they are more agile and alive with greater dexterity. In this analogy, the front of your body is the palm, the back of your body is the back of your hand. Think about how your hand can move, then apply the idea to your entire body. If you could make your core body agile and alive as well- like a third hand- could you make your core function longer and better than it otherwise would?

Having core agility and intelligence through movement leads to greater usefulness and healthfulness than just clenching your core- which makes it strong but locked up and dumb. Let's go over some ways to work on this.

1. Find your diaphragm.

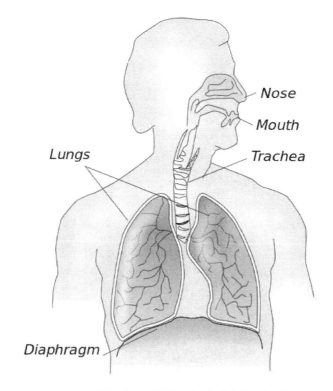

Thank you Wikipedia for this lovely picture.

I admit that this is a toughy at first. It really depends upon how much body awareness you presently have. As I'm sure you already know, the diaphragm is the muscle that runs inside of your body just under your ribcage. Diaphragm, it seems, is ancient

Greek for "partition" and it's primary function is to facilitate breathing.

We want to gain conscious control over the use of the diaphragm as it goes up and down.

This is what leads to the use of the breathing exercises that many martial arts and qigong practices use. There are numerous excellent breathing exercises that are wonderful for your health. Do them, breathing is a good thing and increasing your ability to take in oxygen is a really good thing.

However, I would like to point out is that breathing exercises are a physical practice, not a chi practice. Many people never truly understand chi things as they confuse the physical body with the chi body. But more on this stuff later.

The **first breathing exercise** to play with is to take deep, slow, even breaths that feel like they go all the way down to your belly. Thus the phrase "Belly Breathing." Don't hold your breath anywhere during the process; just be nice and slow and even.

The big idea of this is twofold. First, the more oxygen you can get into your body the better. Second, you can start to get a feel for the movement of the diaphragm.

The **second breathing exercise** to play with is to try to fill up one lung at a time with air. Once again paying attention to what your diaphragm is doing.

The **third breathing exercise** is to try to fill up the bottom half of one or both of your lungs with air and then alternately to try to fill up only the top halves. Or the top half of one and the bottom of the other. Hopefully you get the idea.

The entire objective of these breathing exercises is to, of course, build internal agility and intelligence. Learning to oxygenate your body isn't such a bad thing either.

Interestingly, as you learn to work with the diaphragm by itself, it will fill up the lungs with air anyway.

I've also been told (though again I haven't researched this notion) that by moving your diaphragm you create more space for your heart to operate in, making it healthier.

Do I do breathing exercises? Not very much. The Tai Chi Classics say to only breath naturally. However, I do practice internal diaphragm agilities all of the time. Almost literally. The reason is that we don't want the rhythm of respiration to control all of your movements. You become a slave to that rhythm. Instead, we want the conscious movement of the diaphragm be in control. Let the bottom control the top, not the top controlling the bottom. You will not mess up your breathing and you will have more freedom.

Another exercise you can do is to push your diaphragm down while you lift your head up in a pumping motion. More on this later.

So, learn to wiggle your diaphragm around. Figure it out.

The 6 Steps to Self Mastery. 97

I took this picture at Erhai Lake in China. One of my favorite pictures ever. Ask me some time and I'll tell you the story behind it.

2. Find the lower pelvic muscles.

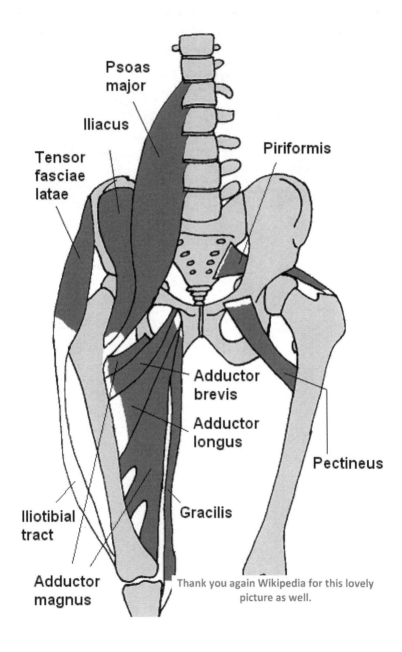

Thank you again Wikipedia for this lovely picture as well.

The first step to this is to "open the kua." Which is fancy pants speak for gently relax and roll out your hips to allow space for greater freedom of movement between them.

This has a lot to do with relaxing and training the iliopsoas muscles, ie, the psoas as well as the iliacus muscles. It is also important to release the piriformis muscle.

Working with these can help you manage lower back pain, scoliosis, sciatica, cramping, bladder issues, as well as upset tummy issues.

Interestingly, the psoas is a very emotionally responsive muscle, fitting into the whole fight, flight, or stand there and get beat up response. Learning to manage and relax these muscles leads to a wonderful sense of calmness and empowerment.

To find these muscles, again begin by gently opening out the hips by gently turning out your knees. Did I mention gently? Don't try to break things off of yourself in the name of fitness.

The next component involves a bit of imagination on your part. Try to shrink and expand the inside of your body on a horizontal line between your hips. Basically, you are trying to find the muscles in question and mess around with them. Try to make them agile and intelligent.

I'll go over some more exercises to do here in the following sections.

> After coming to an understanding of the internal power of movement, you can approach the theory of natural awareness.

3. Shrinking and Expanding.

Shrinking and expanding is a biggy. The basic idea is to work whatever you are training like a pump, only try to do it on a three dimensional level. Try to shrink and expand everything on a spherical level.

Of course, at first you must begin with a line. Pretend that you are holding a rubber band in both hands. Now, pull it apart with both hands, then relax it, and so on. The point is to pull it apart with

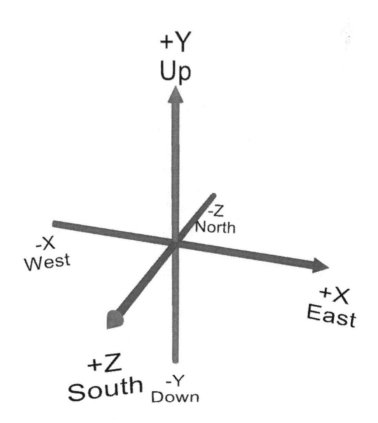

both hands equally, not just one hand.

It is just so when you are shrinking and expanding. When working with a straight line, expand it from both ends, not just one.

To build the 3D model begin with a vertical line that you are shrinking and expanding. Then add in a horizontal line to shrink and expand. Then do both of them together. Next, add in a front to back line to shrink and expand. This way you have an X, Y, and Z plane to work with. Connect these lines into circles. Then let this evolve into a sphere to shrink and expand instead of two dimensional models.

At first this takes a lot of imagination. Just attempt to move whatever body part you are training in this fashion. But do make sure that you are trying to actually move your body. At first you probably will not be able to make things move as you wish, but as you get better your body will become more intelligent.

Begin with wiggling around your diaphragm. Try to have your diaphragm go up while your lower pelvic muscles go down. Make this expand and shrink in a pumping motion.

Then try to have your diaphragm go down while the top of your head goes up. Make this a gentle pumping motion.

Next, push your tailbone down while your head goes up in the same pumping motion.

Follow that by having your diaphragm and lower pelvic muscles go down while your head goes up.

Now, try to add in horizontal expansion between your hips while at the same time doing the vertical shrinking and expanding.

Think of this process as learning to inflate and deflate yourself like a ball.

Also, note that your breathing will follow along with this process, but do not think about your breathing. Remember, we want your internal movement to control the breathing, not the other way around.

There's more to this shrinking and expanding that we'll add on later.

4. **Dan Tien, Huiyin, Mingmen, and Wuji movement.**

The Immortal Emperor Qin Shi Huang. He was immortal until he died around 210 BC from taking pills made from the mercury found in a meteor. At first I laughed, but then remembered that I have some mercury fillings.

We've gone over, in general, what muscles to work with. Hopefully enough for you to have an idea of what you are trying to accomplish without getting too bogged down in useless information. It's the kind of thing that you can over analyze. Not that *you* would do such a thing.

Let's look at this stuff from an oriental chi gong perspective. I find that understanding different perspectives on things is very useful.

In 1567 Emperor Jianjing thought it would be pretty cool to die from the mercury, I mean cinnabar, immortality as well. It seems he figured if he drank the mercury it would work better than pills.

The **Dan Tien** can be translated as "energy center," "elixir field," "sea of chi," or "field of cinnabar." As a funny side story, the Dan Tien is sometimes associated with Chinese Emperors use of Alchemy to seek immortality. Unfortunately, it didn't work out that well. Jiajing Emperor in the Ming Dynasty died from ingesting a lethal dosage of mercury in the supposed "Elixir of Life" conjured by alchemists, as did Emperor Qin Shi Huang. This elixir was supposedly a concoction of cinnabar with mercury in an attempt to become immortal by somehow jump starting the Dan Tien or something. Turns out it wasn't the best of ideas.

Don't worry, we won't be drinking any mercury.

Anyway, there technically are three Dan Tien, upper (the pineal gland in the middle of the forehead), middle (the solar plexus), and the lower (just under your belly button.)

When people talk about the Dan Tien, they generally are referring to the lower Dan Tien. It is located about two or three inches under your belly button.

Next is the **Huiyin Cavity**, which can be translated as "crossing the genitalia." It is located directly at the bottom of your body directly behind your genitalia. Thus the name.

After that is the **Mingmen Cavity**. Mingmen can be translated as "Stone Gate." This point is located on the spine directly below the 2nd lumbar vertebra. Kind of in the middle of your lower back. This is an extremely important point in terms of generating internal power.

And finally we have what is sometimes called the **Wuji** Point, or the true Dan Tien. Let's go with Wuji just to avoid confusion. Of course all of this Chinese is kind of confusing in and of itself, so let's try to be less confusing.

Wuji in this case means "without polarity," or "boundless." The idea being that this point, located in the exact middle of your center of gravity, is said to be the resting place of the first cells to come to life in your body. Supposedly, your first spark of life originally comes from your tailbone and then expands out. It seems that there are originally 8 cells around the tailbone. (Oriental philosophy LOVES numerology, 8 pops up a lot.) It also seems that there are 3 different kinds of energy that are also integrated within this spark giving you consciousness, awareness, and the potential for further growth. Or so I've heard. This gets to be fairly more complicated than this text needs to be.

That's kind of the thing with a lot of this information, there is a great deal of it to sift through. Sometimes it makes sense, sometimes it doesn't, and regardless of how much sense or how little sense it seems to make there is no real way to know what is accurate when you first hear it. Furthermore, how on earth would one discern which cell the spark of life was shot into at the moment of conception? I don't know. I'm just sharing some of the theories.

Anyway, there is a point to all of this.

Circulate your mind in a circle between these points. You start at the Dan Tien in the front, then down to the Huiyin between your legs, and then to the Mingmen in your lower back. Use the Wuji point as the center of the circle.

This rotation is commonly called "Small Circulation."

You can move this circle around the points in any direction you choose, remember, we are working to build core intelligence. The real use of this practice is to get your mind to work with the entire core area. Making sure not to miss the very front, the very bottom, nor the very back.

Me with Baqua Master Shi Sen Lin in China. Nice fellow with really good core agility and power.

5. 3-D Figure eights.

One of the key things to work on is practicing core intelligence and agility drills. Here is one of my favorites. Keeping everything else that we have discussed so far in mind, move your mind inside your abdomen in a figure eight pattern.

Begin with a vertical figure eight, from the bottom torso (the Huiyin) to your diaphragm. Now try to get your body to do the same thing. You should feel like a drunken ox trying to belly dance.

Now repeat the same exercise with a horizontal figure eight. Now do diagonals. In fact, work this figure eight on your core in any three dimensional direction you want.

Now let's add in shrinking and expanding. Instead of moving in a figure eight from just one point, move from two points going in opposite directions. Do this with vertical, horizontal, front to back, diagonal- whatever kind of figure eights you can think of. Make sure to actually move your body.

Here I am with Master Liu Chan Shan in Jilin City, China. He was a key figure in teaching me all kinds of internal power stuff.

Something to remember with all of these core agilities is that you want to gently push the envelope of possible motion. At the same time, don't lock up your muscles at any time. We want to train intelligence, strength, and agile movement- not stiffness and stupidity. In this light, play any games you want with your core agility. We want relaxed agility and intelligence. Any games you can think of are good.

And a great thing about this is that these are core practices you can do no matter where you are and no matter what kind of shape you are in. You can do these very gently if you have physical limitations that require it, and you can make modifications as you need based upon your body. These exercises can be as low key or as intense as you wish.

6. Spherical expansion.

One of the great things about all of these core agilities is that they are the key to long lasting health. Doing these exercises keep your mind active and by moving around the stuff inside of your body you stimulate blood flow and nervous system communication to your organs. You keep your organs alive with vitality and in the right place. Basically, internal intelligence will keep you in better health longer.

Okay now, let's discuss spherical expansion. Once you have done all of the things we have been talking about the next step is to try to expand your entire core area like you are inflating a beach ball. The thing is, you can't contract muscles to do this. In fact, you can't just push out your belly either. That would only be one direction, silly. And to quote one of my favorite movies, we want all positions (in our case, directions)! Are we green? Super Green?

Instead, to get the sphere effect that we are after you must relax and melt everything. Open the hips out, relax the psoas muscles, relax the piriformis muscle, relax everything down there.

With your mind, think of expanding this relaxed area into a sphere. Let that sphere sink down to the bottom of your core mass between your hips. The bigger you can make this relaxed, expanded area the better.

7. Counterweight.

This big relaxed sphere is commonly simply called the Dan Tien, as the Dan Tien is generally thought of as an energy area in the lower abdomen, from the diaphragm to between the hips. Note that in this context we are disregarding the middle and upper dan tien. For our purposes, when we talk about the lower Dan Tien, we will be referring to the entire core area once it has reached this state of melted, expanded intelligence.

This may seem confusing at first, but it's not really. The idea is that at first the Dan Tien, or elixir pool is a very small pool of ninja power. But once you have trained it as we have been discussing it becomes larger, stronger, and more intelligent.

Once you have achieved this large and intelligent Dan Tien, it becomes a counterweight. You have done all of this work to make this area alive, and now you must destroy the work.

Think of it like working on a car. You have to pop the hood to work on the engine, but once you are finished fine tuning it you must close the hood to drive. When you drive the car you don't think about all of the inner workings of the engine, you just use it.

Dan Tien power is much the same. You have worked under the hood on your core, now step back and put it to work.

That work is as a counterweight. Use the melted core mass as a counterweight, use your expanded spine or Central equilibrium as the pivot post, the arm is, well, your arm, and the load is whatever you are moving.

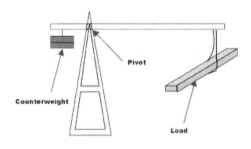

This is a Wikipedia crane.

This is what it means to move from your core. Do not try to use the pivot to lift something as most people do. This would physically translate to trying to pick things up with your shoulders- as most people do.

In fact, looking at where the pivot is, you can see why it is so important to melt the shoulders. If they carry tension they reduce the effectiveness of the counterweight, making everything weaker.

You also don't want to have the shoulder "welded" to the body as you will sometimes hear. If you were to weld the arm to the center post your scale, crane, or whatever machine you were using the counterweight for, your machine wouldn't move worth a hoot and certainly wouldn't pick anything up very well. Much is the same with body. If you weld your shoulders you kill the intelligent use and power of the rest of your body.

Therefore, you need to let your shoulders relax and be empty but attached to the torso.

Step 4: Work with the Earth.

Now we're getting somewhere. Earth power. This is kind of a big deal. The base concept is a very simple one. Remember the scale or crane with a counterweight from the last chapter? Don't you think it would work better if you put the crane on the ground for a foundation? This is the beginning of the concept, though to be honest it isn't really that simple.

Dum dum dum dum. It's the Earth!

1. The bottom of your feet.

You'll want to work towards using the bottom of your feet to control what your hands do. Therefore, you should work on making your feet as intelligent as possible.

Use them to create spiraling power for the entire body. Use them to add downward pressure to create earth reaction force (more on that next section). Use them to shift your weight and balance.

You will often read that you should have your feet flat on the floor based on a four corners model. This is a good beginning idea while you are working on structure, but as always once you have that you need to destroy it. We don't want your feet to be bricks, make them more dexterous like lions paws.

Now work on building agility and intelligence with your feet. But there is a caveat; this intelligence needs to be built with the idea of controlling the rest of the body- not a localized intelligence.

To do this, work the floor. Put gentle force into the earth and feel the upward reaction force. When you push down into the earth, it pushes you up. Play with the subtlety of this concept.

Also, work pushing and pulling with your feet on the floor to create spiraling power. Push one foot forward and the other one back to turn your body, kind of like how you turn a steering wheel. Keep your body loose, open, and empty with your head up.

The smarter you make your feet, the higher level your ninja skillz will become. Remember, the bottom controls the top!

2. Reaction force.

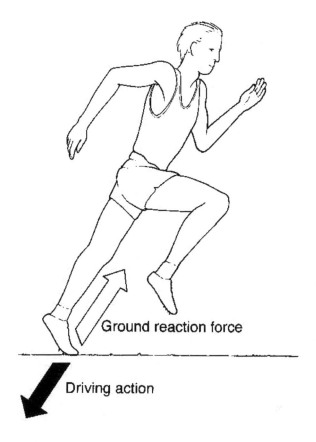

Let's talk a bit more about this earth reaction force thing. This is also often just called earth power. The first part of this is to melt, have what they call "chi goes through." More on that in a minute. The next thing is to have a large, melted core. Dan Tien Power.

Now, melt the Dan Tien down to the floor.

Put your mind onto the bottom of your feet and think about how it interacts with the earth. Begin by bending and straightening your legs in a circular motion. At first it is really easy to put your mind on your quadriceps (the big muscles on the front of your legs). Don't put your mind there, stay focused on the bottom of your feet. Your legs should be springy and agile, but let the force go through them into the ground.

Now as you do this motion, think about how you are really pushing into the earth, giving it force, and then relaxing that giving of force. This is a lot like you are jumping up, only you don't actually jump. Instead of propelling your body up, become sensitive enough to create the force you would need to go up, but just have the energy go up your back without actually having your body come up. Play putting power into the earth to create an upward reaction force.

This is really important to figure out. Work on it.

3. Chi goes through.

This is all about force management. When you experience an incoming force, let it go through your body into the earth. You can then use the force that your opponent gives you to fuel the earth reaction force. You no longer have to push into the earth yourself- the other guy will do it for you.

To do this, you need to be completely melted. If there is something solid in your body the incoming force will get stuck in it, and you will not have chi goes through. Melt, melt, and then melt some more.

Next, you will have to use your mind and intention to guide the incoming force into the floor. Have the chi go down the front of your body, then you will use earth reaction force to have chi go up the back.

This is a simple concept that is difficult to get right enough. You may need to seek the help of a massage therapist or an acupuncturist to help you with this chi flow and melting stuff. Once you figure out what you are doing you will not need as much help from others, but to begin with you may need help recognizing where you are blocked up.

As always, your mind is the key. Your mind leads the chi, and the chi leads your body. Train your mind to guide chi or force down your body and into the floor.

In this context, think of chi as force. However, as you get to a higher level we will begin to discuss chi in a different light. It's not so much that the reality of chi will change, it's just that your perception of what it is will change.

"Chi goes through" is often best practiced with the use of partner testing. Just have somebody gently press anywhere on your body and try to allow that force to flow into the floor. Then go practice without a partner and try to pretend that you are allowing that force to flow into the floor. Then go back to the partner again. This is one of those test then practice things.

In summary of earth power, let the incoming force go down to the floor, use your feet to manipulate it, and give energy into the earth to create counter force back up so that you can then guide it into the other person.

Step 5: Heaven and Earth Circulation.

Tai Chi guys always get pretty geeked when they get to talk about Heaven and Earth Power. One of my friends, who reminds me of David Van Driessen, is always going on about this stuff.

Sometimes fancy Tai Chi dudes will get into arguments about which is better, earth power or heaven power? Once again I am greatly amused by how angry peaceful people can get.

Sometimes people get so busy trying to be right that they forget to think.

The heaven or earth argument is silly because of one simple thing: the concept of yin and yang. Most people are a little befuddled by yin and yang, thinking them to be only opposites. The average thinking is that the concept entails day vs night, good vs bad, Star Trek vs Star Wars, black vs white, 45 vs 9, etc.

This is incorrect due to the lack of interaction. Yin and Yang are opposing forces, but opposing forces taking place at the same time and interacting in the

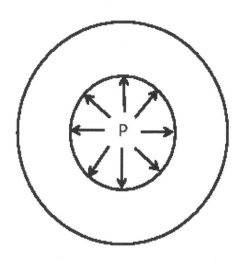

same space. It's kind of like inflating a ball. When you stick the needle in the ball to inflate it you cannot only inflate one half of the ball. The air pressure has force to inflate the ball equally in the entire sphere (see how it suddenly becomes a 3-D model? And you without your 3 D glasses.) There is force going in opposite directions at the same time.

Furthermore, there is an interaction of not only the internal force of the ball, but also an interaction of the internal force of the ball vs. the external atmospheric pressure on the ball.

Now add in the idea that these forces are constantly moving and interacting. This is where you get the typical Yin/Yang logo from. Check out how it compares to the view of a hurricane. Similar? Why yes, yes it is. You might even say that it is an expression of the same principle. Hmmm....

Pretty nifty.

Here's how this pertains to heaven and earth power. You use earth power to create heaven power.

What you will learn how to do is use your power to stimulate the earth power, which then interacts with the heaven power.

Let's look at how this whole thing works. We will begin with how to generate internal power in your body and then move on to how you can use that to jump start the rest of the process.

What you will end up with is incredible power. We will maximize the power that your body can generate and then combine it with the earth and the sky. This is commonly called combination force.

Let's get to it!

1. Counterweight down.

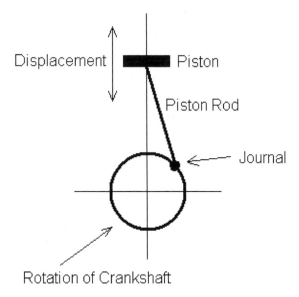

We shall begin our journey with counterweight power. Hopefully from our previous discussion of this you already have a pretty good idea of what this is all about. The basic idea is to build the counterweight up to be as large and intelligent as possible. Then let it melt. This will give you a very solid yet relaxed sense of core stability. But now you need to melt it down into the earth.

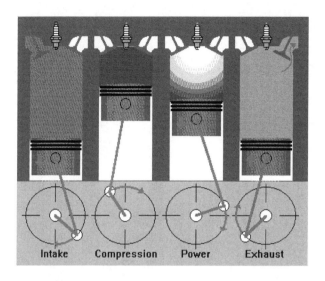

It's kind of like a piston system. Check out this diagram of a 4 stroke piston system. Only, in place of the piston, think of it as your core mass. Then, instead of the piston bar, think of downward chi or force, and then, for the sake of your body, think of the circle or wheel as covering your entire body. In other words, the piston should be inside of the wheel, not on top of it.

Of course this is an analogy in an attempt to get an idea into your head. The idea is that your Dan Tien, or core mass, should relax and this relaxation should then go all the way down to the bottom of your feet. This works as a counterweight for incoming force (something has to push the piston down), and you allow the force to carry down through your body into the floor. But you don't just dump it there, you use this downward force to rotate the crankshaft --which can be likened to where your feet press into

the floor, creating upward reaction force from the feet up the spine to be led by the head.

The Dan Tien serves as a counterweight, and then as a piston when connected into the rest of the body. This piston helps drive chi down into the earth, which is then driven up the back. Down the front, up the back. Once you can figure this out you should forget about the counterweight, destroy it, and work on working the earth reaction force up. Speaking of which....

2. Earth reaction force up.

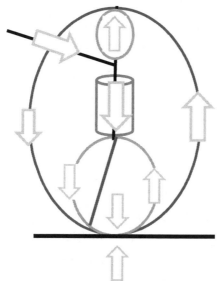

Once you have the feel for using your core intelligently, then as a counterweight, then as a piston, you can move your focus away from it on down to the floor. All of the core stuff is designed to help you **not** hold yourself up so you can gain more earth reaction force. Do not carry yourself, nor the incoming force.

The big idea is to use the incoming force of your opponent. Use incoming force to press the core downwards like a piston and then use reaction force from the ground up the back of your body, and then guide it where ever you want- generally back into whatever is pushing you. In this way, the force coming into your body combines with the force that you can generate and then is guided right back into whatever you want to guide it back into. Therefore, the core and the feet go down, making the head go up.

However, now it is time to forget all that stuff. Just do this. Think of the incoming force as going down in the front of your body, then use your feet to create spiraling and reaction force that goes up the back of your body. This force is then guided by your head.

Remember that the incoming force can be anything. It can be a physical force, like somebody pushing on you, or it could be any other kind of force. This concept of internal power works against physical force, emotional force, stress related force, whatever!

3. The Head is suspended.

If the power from the whole thing really comes from earth reaction force, the head at the top of the model will guide where the force should go. If we go back to the car jack analogy, you have to actually put the jack under your car to pick it up. You can crank the jack next to the car all you want; it won't be picking anything up.

Your head guides the long lever power generated by your center equilibrium, and then guides the upward force generated by the use of earth reaction force. So what ends up happening is that the power that is put into you from whatever is giving you force (a person pushing you, your boss yelling at you, your kids drawing on the walls, whatever) is transferred into the earth. The earth then gives reaction force back up through your spine that then lifts your head. Your head then guides the power back into whatever pushed in the first place. This is where the idea of "hold the body like a perfectly balanced scale" comes from.

This soon will turn into the concept of chi goes down and spirit goes up. We'll get into that in the next section on chi body.

4. Connecting the Hands.

One of the common questions I get from students is what to do with the hands. How do you connect them to the internal power? You want your arms to be empty. Think of a wolf's legs. A wolf will walk about 30 miles a day, and if you look at them their legs are empty, with what we call "chi goes through."

More specifically, relax your shoulders and neck completely. Use the Yijin Jing stretches we will go over later to develop the attachment of the arms to the body mass via where the back connects to your armpit at the bottom of your shoulder- your lats.

Then forget that part.

Next, think of the palms of your hands connecting inward to the diaphragm, then the diaphragm in and down to the mingmen (lower back). Your hands, diaphragm and mingmen will create sort of a backwards vortex. Keep your shoulders and neck empty and your head up.

Use the feet to control the hands. Think of your hands and feet as being the same, like a four legged animal. Then use the movement of the feet to manipulate the movement of the hands. If the feet press into the earth, the hands go up. If the feet suck on the earth, the hands go down. Use this practice in conjunction with spiraling power from the feet to make the connection to the hands very intelligent.

As for your hands themselves, the back expands out and your palms suck in. As you get better at this you will see a circle develop in the middle of your hand.

Keep your hands empty, like a lions paws, but transferring force through. There should be no physical tension in the hands, use the internal power to give them shape. Remember, the chi from the hands goes into the body, not out and away from it.

If you make a fist, work on expanding it, the inside sucks and the outside expands. Make it feel like you are wearing incredible hulk boxing gloves.

All in all, your hands should look light and empty, but should be attached to the core via the diaphragm and mingmen. Then down to the earth, where the hands are played by the feet.

5. Yin and yang direction.

Yin and yang is a concept that most westerners get totally wrong. We generally think of yin and yang as being opposites- black and white, water and vinegar, men and women, dogs and cats, Gandalf and Sarumon... you get the idea.

This is almost right, but significantly wrong. Yin and Yang are opposites, but the relevance of them is that they interact. It is not about having one or the other, nor are they separate. They work together to create. I know, we touched on this a little earlier in the book, but it becomes really important right about here.

In terms of our model for Earth Reaction Force coming up, we need to understand the concept of Yin and Yang reasonably well. Look back over what was discussed earlier, but the general idea is that we want to have opposing force working together to create shrinking and expanding, volume, and so on.

How this applies here is pretty simple. When your core (counterweight, piston) and feet go down, your head goes up. There is a shrinking and expanding motion along with the rotating motion. The front of your body goes down, the back goes up. The core goes down the head goes up. The jade pillow (knob on the back of your head) goes up, and the mingmen (lower back) goes down. The feet give force to the ground; the ground gives force up to the head. The external force gives force into you, and you let it drive all of this other stuff happening to give force back to whatever is pushing on you. In fact, you combine the force generated by your inner workings with the force given to you externally, thereby greatly increasing your power output to give back! The ability to do this is called "being alive," or the "predator body." Every part of your body has intelligence, can shrink and expand, has flexibility, and can move and work together. Just like a predatory animal might move.

Don't be selfish, be a giver! If somebody gives you force, take it so you can give them back at least twice what they give you!

Words of Wisdom from an unlikely source....

BEAVIS: yeah, heh heh... hey butt-head, how come like, some stuff sucks, but then like, some stuff is pretty cool? heh heh...

BUTT-HEAD: uh... huh huh... well, huh huh... if nothing sucked, and like, everything was cool all the time, then it's like, how would you know it was cool? huh huh...

Step 6: Finding Your Chi Body.

Chi is a fascinating thing. The common mistake in the western mind is to attempt to liken Chi to some type of physical process, like breathing or core movement exercises. Don't get me wrong, breathing exercises and core exercises are very important- but they are physical body and not chi body exercises.

> **Richard Feynman**
> "It is important to realize that in physics today, we have no knowledge what energy is. We do not have a picture that energy comes in little blobs of a definite amount."

So what is chi? In a word, change. In more words, a change in energy, or a change of state. It would seem that chi is the act of transforming energy. Going from potential energy to kinetic energy to force.

Wikipedia says, *"In physics, the term energy describes the capacity to produce certain changes within a system, without regard to limitations in transformation imposed by Entropy. Changes in total energy of systems can only be accomplished by adding or subtracting energy from them, as energy is a quantity which is conserved, according to the first law of thermodynamics. According to special relativity, changes in the energy of systems will also coincide with changes in the system's mass, and the total amount of mass of a system is a measure of its energy."*

The way chi was first described to me that made any sense was with a few analogies.

- Air does not have chi, but wind has chi.
- Not the seasons themselves, but the changing of them is chi.
- Ice does not have chi, but changing it to water has chi.
- Still water does not have chi, but a flowing river has chi.

Stuff like that.

Basically, chi is when something changes. It is the energy of change. Which, if you look at the

> ### Zen Master Sêng-chao/Sõjõ
> Heaven and earth and I are of the same root.
>
> The ten-thousand things and I are of one substance.
>
> (僧肇 384-414)

definition provided above- energy is the change within a system- so there you have it I guess. It is the change of speed, volume, or mass- all interacting together.

Once again, this is all about interaction. Chi is not about the mountain nor the stream, it is about how they interact as part of a system. Remember, the entire concept of Yin and Yang is about interaction. This is a theory attempted to describe the way the universe works. In this regard, chi is not this or that, it is the change and interaction that needs to take place. It has volume, it has movement, it has shrinking and expanding, it has depth and breadth….

Do not think of chi as a thing to be located and isolated- it is the very opposite.

However, I didn't start passing tests until I started thinking of chi a little bit differently still.

Think of chi as the changing fabric from which the universe is constructed. It is constantly moving and flowing, evolving and changing, shrinking and expanding. Do not think of it as a two dimensional graph, think of chi as vibrant and alive and with three dimensional volume.

But there is more. Chi is the fabric, but it is not the seamstress. It will bend to your will and take the shape it is given.

There is an old statement that should become words to live by:

The mind leads the chi, and the chi leads the body.

This is a pretty big deal and we'll discuss this more in a minute, but first….

The three fates. Who is your seamstress?

1. Find your ghost.

> ### Pierre Teilhard de Chardin
> We are not human beings having a spiritual experience. We are spiritual beings having a human experience.

To begin to figure out the chi body you must begin to think about it differently. The best way to do it is to think about your chi body as an actual different body. You have your physical body, and you have your chi body. They are different bodies, different aspects of you.

Chen Fake. Famous Tai Chi dude.

To train the chi body, you must train the chi body. The big mistake most people make is they say they are going to train chi, but then start doing something physical. Train your chi and the body will follow.

To begin with, your chi

body and physical body are intertwined. The first thing to do here is to try to distinguish them. To train the chi body you must look for it.

I'm afraid that I cannot tell you exactly how to do that. Do the exercises listed here and try to be empty. Try to find the ghost within your physical body. When you do, try to move it instead of your physical self. Let the physical follow your ghost.

It's ghost me!

2. Physical should be loose, open, empty, and relaxed.

This is where it becomes especially important for you to melt away your body. Your body should be loose open and sunk. Any tension in the body will mess up the chi body. Not because the chi depends upon the lack of tension- but you do! Your mind, focus, and intent will go to the tension that you have.

Remember that your tension is mental and emotional much more than physical. The tightness in your shoulders got there because of stress. Even if you have old injuries, the tension and chi blockage there is because you have hung on to it. I'm not saying that the physical injury will magically go away with chi training, but the blockage of chi will wear down and go away.

Keep your body empty and relaxed, let it be open and empty. Your mind is what makes it tense up, so to do this you must give yourself permission to relax and melt.

3. Chi goes down, spirit goes up.

In the physical model we talked about how force goes down into the earth, and then the earth reaction force goes back up to the head. That is the beginning of this concept, but now there is more.

I would recommend that for chi training you change your mental analogy from a piston engine to bigger, more power, more natural things. I like to think of a waterfall going down in the front and a tsunami in the back. Traditionally, in front of you is yin and is often likened to a stream, while behind you is yang and is likened to a mountain. This is where the feng shui thing about having your house positioned with a mountain behind you and a stream in front came from.

Below you will find a basic diagram of directional feng shui called the Baqua, or eight trigrams. I'm sticking this in here just to give you an idea of how to begin to think about chi, it's interaction, and the relationships that are influenced. I wouldn't get too tied up in this stuff- for our purposes just note that it's all about relationships and interactions.

Directions, elements, cycles of nature, even family relationships can be thought of in terms of how chi flows and pertains to them.

卦名 Name	自然 Nature	季节 Season	性情 Personality	家族 Family	方位 Direction	意義 Meaning
離 Li	火 Fire	Summer	Clinging	中女 Middle Daughter	南 South	Rapid movement, radiance, the sun.
坤 Kun	地 Earth	Summer	Receptive	母 Mother	西南 Southwest	Receptive energy, that which yields.
兌 Dui	澤 Lake	Autumn	Joyous	少女 Youngest Daughter	西 West	Joy, satisfaction, stagnation.
乾 Qian	天 Heaven	Autumn	Creative	父 Father	西北 Northwest	Expansive energy, the sky.
坎 Kan	水 Water	Winter	Abysmal	中男 Middle Son	北 North	Danger, rapid rivers, the abyss, the moon.

艮 Gen	山 Mountain	Winter	Still	少男 Youngest Son	東北 Northeast	Stillness, immovability.
震 Zhen	雷 Thunder	Spring	Arousing	長男 Eldest Son	東 East	Excitation, revolution, division.
巽 Xun	風 Wind	Spring	Gentle	長女 Eldest Daughter	東南 Southeast	Gentle penetration, flexibility.

Once again, thank you Wikipedia for this lovely chart and picture.

For our purposes we do not want a mountain behind us as they don't move very well. We want a more alive yang energy, so we'll go with a tsunami.

Wiki pic. Ride the wave!

Now when you think of the rotation process in your body (the counterweight, then piston driven engine thing), think of the earth under your feet as the living earth that you are interacting with, not just a matter of playing with force, but think of the earth as a living, breathing entity. When you play the earth, give it not only force, but also interact with it. In your mind become a part of it. When you give it chi, accept the chi it gives back. Mix this chi with the tsunami force behind you, that then mixes with the sky over you, then the waterfall in front of you.

Ignore your body. Do not try to analyze this process, try to feel it. Try to become it. You can't drive your car by tinkering with the engine. You cannot enjoy a movie by analyzing the production quality. You cannot fall in love by questioning the hormones. You have to **FEEL** it.

Bruce Lee, Enter the Dragon

"Don't think, feel! It is like a finger pointing a way to the moon. Don't concentrate on the finger or you will miss all that heavenly glory. Do you understand?" I like to say this in a Chinese accent. It adds.

Three bodies. You must train your physical body and then melt it. You must find your chi body, and then sink it. You must find your spirit body, and let it rise up.

This feels like you are standing in a waterfall and then step back. The waterfall is still going down, but you are not in it. If somebody is pushing on your hands, you can transfer that force down like a waterfall, but then your mind goes up and back, out of the force. So you are aware of the force going down through your body, but you are not part of it.

What is spirit? It is not physical and it is not chi. Physical is solid, chi is light and fuller than physical, and spirit is lighter still. Defining spirit for you is like trying to tell a blind man what the color green looks like. I cannot describe it to you further than I have. But know that it exists, is a body that you have, and when you feel it you will know what I mean.

The physical melts, the chi sinks, and the spirit rises.

At first the mind and chi are inside of the body. Then the body is inside of the chi. Then the chi is inside of the mind.

The true function of internal power training is to refine yourself so much that you can clearly distinguish the three bodies, then to become agile and alive with your physical body, but also with your chi body, and mind body.

Mind body and spirit body are fairly interchangeable at this time. Some will get persnickety about this, but whatever. When you can feel what I am talking about you will see that it isn't so relevant which words you use to define things. None of them are quite right anyway and the layers and levels that you create to communicate the experience are not actually there. They are just attempts to verbalize something that can only be felt.

Do not get stuck in analysis paralysis, which is easy to do. Also, don't get too philosophical. Keep it simple and practice refinement.

4. You should feel light.

"*Before Enlightenment chop wood carry water, after Enlightenment, chop wood carry water.*" Zen saying.

"*Before I had studied Zen for thirty years, I saw mountains as mountains, and waters as waters. When I arrived at a more intimate knowledge, I came to the point where I saw that mountains are not mountains, and waters are not waters. But now that I have got its very substance I am at rest. For it's just that I see mountains once again as mountains, and waters once again as waters.*"[13] Ch'uan Teng Lu, 22. (The Way of Zen 126)

Once you have

- Proper body alignment,
- An alive spine,
- Activated your core,
- Played the earth,
- Heaven and earth power
- and Chi body

You should feel light but unstoppable. Empty yet full. Your spirit and consciousness should feel raised, your chi should feel sunk, your body should feel gone. You should feel light, agile, and alive!

A common mistake people make is to sink the chi and play the earth, but with the idea of rooting down. Everything is down, down, down. They seem to forget that the reason a tree sends down roots is so that it can grow upward!

Be empty, be light, be agile. Make your body like a predatory animal- heavy yet empty, light but full, relaxed but powerful. Intelligent but calm.

Activate every cell in your body. Make your self-knowledge of such a high level that you feel completely clean, completely pure, completely alive!

When you use earth power to raise your spirit you will begin to feel this. You will feel nothing, yet be completely centered and grounded. You will feel completely free.

This comes from finding your equilibrium. You cannot be too yin nor too yang. You need to find the perfect balance of the physical body, chi body, and spirit body.

Your body should be loose, open, and empty, your chi should be sunk from the waist to the earth, your spirit should be raised. Your mind should be clear and focused. Speaking of mind, that's kind of a big deal as well. Let's look into it.

> ### A.A. Milne
>
> "'Supposing a tree fell down, Pooh, when we were underneath it?' 'Supposing it didn't,' said Pooh. After careful thought, Piglet was comforted by this."

5. Yi is the key.

Yi is mind, intention, and focus all wrapped up into one. I like to express this concept in three different levels in an attempt to communicate the point. You can think of these with different words, whatever you would like, it is the concept that is important.

First is focus. This is your ability to have your mind on only one thing. Let's say you are learning to drive your car. You have to focus on each individual step. You focus on which pedal to push, how to turn the wheel, how to try to judge the distance to a stop or a turn…. Each little thing requires you to focus inside of your mind. This tends to take place inside of your head while you are looking out. What I mean to say is that your consciousness is inside of your head.

Second is Intention. This is where you can put your focus or your mind outside of your head. Just like you can reach out with your hand to touch something- you can reach out with your mind the same way. I'm not suggesting that you are becoming telekinetic, just that you can expand your awareness.

To use the driving analogy, this is like when you are driving down the road and see the Tasty Freeze. You then subconsciously decide to turn in to get a sundae, without even verbalizing the idea inside of your mind. Your intention goes to the tasty freeze, your mind is already there. You are able to turn into the parking lot without thinking about distance, nor how to use the controls of the car- your body is in harmony with that so you don't need to even consider it. It happens without you thinking about it. You are able to turn in without judging distance, nor even considering that you should.

All of this happens because your intent is already at the Tasty Freeze, your mind is not in the car. It is not confined to your head. Your mind and intent are on the target.

Third is awareness. This is where you have intent as I have defined it here, but your mind is not focused like a laser on just one thing. You have that level of focus, but you are also aware of everything else around you.

This is like when a football quarterback steps up in the pocket before getting hit in the back by a guy he couldn't see, but he could feel. It is when a basketball player passes the ball to somebody behind him without even looking.

To use the driving analogy again, when you are turning into tasty freeze you are still aware of everything else around you. You stop with traffic before you get to the turn because you are aware. You know there is a car in the lane next to you because you are aware. You are focused on your goal, but also know everything around you, even if you are not actively thinking about it. In fact, for you to be at the level of awareness, you are not actively thinking about anything.

The reason I am using a driving analogy is that I'll bet you have already reached this level of mind with the operation of your car.

Now we want to reach this same level with the operation of yourself. Yi is all of these things put together-focus, intent, awareness. It is the ability to have your mind lead and everything else follows.

Your mind leads the chi, and the chi leads the body (and the body leads the car.)

Learn to move your yi around. Train your focus/intention/awareness mind in all that you do. Have it lead the chi in your body. Have it control the earth power, the tsunami power, the waterfall power. Have it manipulate the counterweight power. Have it guide the tension from your body to become loose, open, and empty.

Yi is the key to making all of this work. Train your mind to be aware, alive, and agile.

6. Yi is bigger than your physical body.

We want your yi to be bigger than your physical body. At first the mind and chi are inside of your body. Then your body and mind are inside of the chi. And finally, the body and chi are inside of the mind.
In reality, you never really train chi, just yi. Chi will follow yi. But you have to train it to do so just as you would train a dog to follow your instruction.

Do not limit the scope of your mind to be within the confines of your physical body. Your mind body awareness is not limited to your physical self.

Have you ever seen a toddler want to go across the room, get up to run and fall down? I have a theory that this is because its mind and body are not yet very well unified. Its mind is already across the room, but it left the body behind.

As adults we have better unity, so you can project your intention and still have your body follow.

The point, however, is that your sense of self need not be limited to the flesh. Your perceived area that your consciousness takes up can be much larger than your skin.

I'm not talking about astral projection. That is the act of totally leaving the body, breaking the connection with only a tether to connect back. I'm talking about having a unified body, chi, spirit connection that is guided by the yi. Each body makes the lesser do stuff.

Practice having your mind be bigger than your body. The way you do this is to let your mind melt, just as you did with your body. Let it relax. You will find that it is not confined by the physical. Let your awareness fill the entire room.

If you go outside let your mind melt and relax. Let your awareness expand to whatever you are around in nature. Make conscious contact with your environment. Become a part of it.

In Chinese martial arts there is a saying that when you have third hand power (this is when your core and torso are intelligent, just like your hands) your body will live as long as your hand (the theory being that peoples organs tend to fail before then manual dexterity does). When you have natural awareness power, you live as long as nature does. At least for as long as you are connected to it.

So in theory, you can be immortal for a few minutes.

I admit that this is a pretty and poetic notion. I'm not sure if I would consider it to be a quest for immortality in the Gilgamesh sense. Rather I think it is a quest for immortality in the moment, to be completely whole, aware, and alive in that one very instant and in that instant to see connected eternity.

Enlightenment is nothing more than to see what truly is. Not what you want to see, not what you think you should see, not what you were told you would see. Just to see.

That is the "natural awareness" that the classic writings speak of.

I know this is more of a yoga picture, but the sentiment still applies.

The first time I experienced this was in Jilin, China while I was working with Lui Chan Shan. He had me stand in the Zhen Zhuan "Standing Pole" position for four or five hours. At first I was good. Then I started to get fatigued. Then very fatigued. Then I thought I was going to die right there. After that my body literally gave up from exhaustion and I stopped hurting. I went beyond the physical and started to cry. I was cutting through the layers of myself, one by one, seeing things about myself I did not care to see.

Then I found a certain peace.

At this moment I saw what it is to be enlightened, to be aware. It is only to see what is and accept it. Nothing more.

The Daily Workout.

Here is a suggestion for what to do on a daily basis for your actual training session. Everything you have read up to now is what you should be doing while you are doing these exercises. None of the things in this book are philosophy, everything here is practice.

The difference is pretty simple. A philosophy is an idea that you get to ponder and pontificate about, but a practice is something you are actually doing.

Everything here is practice.

In review, here are the six steps to awesome ninja powers.

Step 1: Align your body.

Step 2: Activate your spine.

Step 3: Build Core agility.

Step 4: Play the Earth.

Step 5: Heaven and Earth Power.

Step 6: Find your Chi Body.

These six steps are of course, only the beginning. There is much, much more. But you've got to start somewhere! Oh, look me up on Youtube for a video of some of these. It's hard to follow movements via photo.

Let's get to it!

1. **Part one: Daily alignment.**

These alignment exercises are technically called Yijin Jing, which can be translated as Bone/Ligament/Tendon Changing exercises. Often times we will translate them as Spiraling Power stretches.

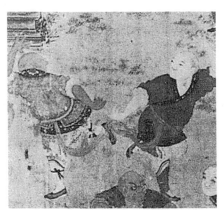

Picture on the Wall at the Shaolin Temple, or so Wikipedia says. Though come to think of it, I do remember seeing something like this when I visited the temple. I mostly remember the cool statues everywhere and the lame tourist trap appeal the place now has.

According to Wikipedia….

Purposes of Yijin Jing

The basic purpose of Yijin Jing is to turn flaccid and frail sinews and tendons into strong and sturdy ones. The movements of Yijin Jing are at once vigorous and gentle. Their performance calls for a unity of will and strength, i.e. using one's will to direct the exertion of muscular strength. It is coordinated with breathing. Better muscles and tendons means better health and shape, more resistance, flexibility, and endurance. It is obtained as follows:

- *postures influence the static and nervous structure of the body*
- *stretching muscles and sinews affects organs, joints, meridians and Qi*
- *torsion affects metabolism and Jing production*
- *breathing produces more and better refined Qi*
- *active working gives back balance and strength to body and mind (brain, nervous system and spirit).*

As you read this wiki article, remember that the mind leads the chi and the chi leads the body. Breathing is an excellent exercise, but breath does not control chi as it is a physical process. Yijin Jing is good for chi circulation as it prepares the body to circulate chi more efficiently, but you cannot use a physical process to control a chi process.

You could think of it like this. Yijin Jing builds a good highway system, but doesn't put the cars on it, nor does it give the cars direction on where to go.

There is something cool about doing an ancient exercise routine that was the secret key to making the Shaolin monks so tough.

I do admit that we are not doing all 18 of these, but I didn't want to as I would rather focus more on chi building exercises for our time spent. And no, these are specifically bone/ligament/tendon building exercises, not chi exercises. Do not confuse the two. These are excellent and important, but not the same.

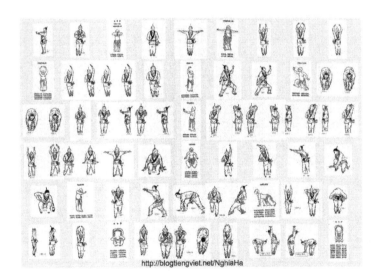

From the wiki page on Yijin JIng.

a. Press your hands.

Stand with your feet shoulder width apart, maybe a slight touch duck footed.
- ✓ Lift the back of your head,
- ✓ Let out your lower back (mingmen),
- ✓ Elongate the spine,

- ✓ Shoulders back and down. No fold in the front and no scapula in the back. No scapula means that you have them rolled under so if someone were to touch your back they would not feel a bump where the bone sticks out.
- ✓ Gently roll the hips out by gently rolling the knees out.
- ✓ Stand so your weight is evenly distributed on both feet, do not roll your feet, nor be front or back heavy. Use the bubbling well point in the middle of your foot for reference.
- ✓ Press your hands together in front of you. Use your feet to create the pressure between the hands, do not use your shoulders- keep them empty.
- ✓ Breath deeply but naturally.
- ✓ Apply these principles to all of the alignment exercises.

b. Spiraling and reaching.

Keep your feet facing forward, spiral with one hand reaching to the front with the other hand reaching to the back. Look behind you.

- ✓ Spiral from the feet. Have one foot give pressure on the floor forward, and the other backward. This will make your entire body spiral.
- ✓ Allow this spiraling to go all the way up to your head and out through your fingertips.
- ✓ Elongate the spine.
- ✓ Keep your shoulders down, no scapula.
- ✓ Reach with both hands as if you are trying to touch the opposing walls.
- ✓ Do both sides, making sure to spiral from the bottom of the feet and allow the spiral to go all the way up your body.

c. Hang like a monkey, Reach behind.

Face forward. Go up on the balls of both feet. Only pick your heels up off of the ground by a couple of inches, don't go crazy. Stick one arm up in the air with your fingers reach to the sky. Push the other arm down to the floor. You should look like a monkey hanging by one arm.

- ✓ Focus on opening your ribcage on the side of the upward reaching arm.
- ✓ Do not actually reach with the arm, keep it connected at the shoulder. Reach with the opening of the ribcage.
- ✓ Elongate the spine, keep the head up.
- ✓ Do both sides.

The 6 Steps to Self Mastery. 179

For the reaching behind part, take the arm that is extended upward and bend it behind your back so your elbow is extended upward and the hand is down. Bend the arm that would be pointing down the same way. Do not grab your hands behind your back, this takes away some of the dynamic tension we want.

- ✓ Elongate the spine.
- ✓ Open the ribcage on the upward reaching side and close the ribcage on the downward side.
- ✓ Look at your lifted heels on side downward elbow side.
- ✓ Do this on both sides.

d. Neck looseners.

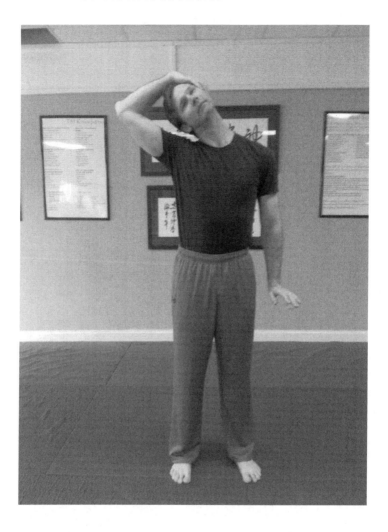

Neck flexibility is one of these things that sneakily waves goodbye. One day when I was about 30 I realized that I could barely turn my head to back up my car! Let's work on that.

Stand like you do in exercise one. With your right hand grab the left side of your head and gently pull it to the right side. Then do the other side.

- ✓ Make sure that you are being gentle!
- ✓ Keep your shoulders down and back.
- ✓ Keep your back straight.

> **Chang San-Feng**
>
> In motion the whole body should be light and agile,
>
> with all parts of the body linked
>
> as if threaded together.

Now, with the pads of your thumbs, grab under the occipital ridge at the back of your skull. Gently lift straight up.

- ✓ Stay looking straight ahead. Don't look down- this isn't that stretch.
- ✓ Let the lower back relax, let the mingmen (middle of the lower back) relax out.
- ✓ This is a total spinal stretch; you should feel it all the way down to the tailbone as you get good at it.

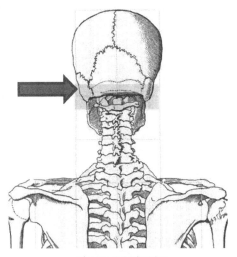

The Occipital Ridge.

Chang San-Feng

The postures should be without defect,

without hollows or projections from the proper

alignment;

e. Touch your toes.

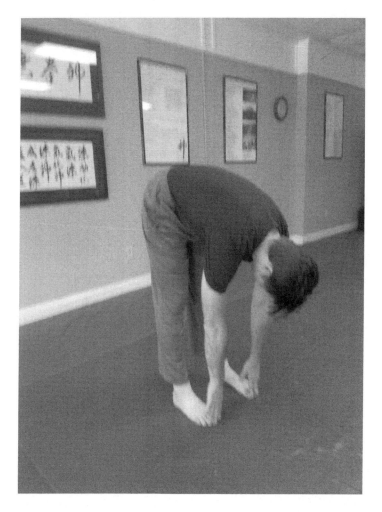

Touching your toes is like eating eggs, it goes in and out of style. People argue about what the best method is and if it's even good for you. Well, all methods are fine so long as you don't hurt your back and yes, it's good for you. The idea is to stretch the backs of your legs, which is important. Do it however you want, but here's the way I do it.

Put your feet together and straighten your knees. Slowly bend forward to touch towards your toes as far as you can.

- ✓ Feel the stretch in the back of your legs, but don't try to break anything off by going too far.
- ✓ Don't bounce, go down gently and relax into the stretch a little bit more with every exhale.
- ✓ Be gentle coming back up. Sometimes I'll walk my hands up the front of my legs on the way up so as to not strain my lower back.
- ✓ Do not strain your lower back.

f. Stand on one foot.

This one is actually a lot like the better known standing tree exercise in Yoga. I suspect the similar roots of the two arts accounts for this. The reason that I like these exercises a little bit better than Yoga (a personal preference) is that I like the dynamic tension and spiraling power as well as the fact that these do not require a lot of the more dramatic stretching Yoga does. Plus, Shaolin monks are cool, like old school Jedi.

Stand on one foot. Press your hands together in front of you like in exercise one. Pick up the other foot and put in on the inner thigh of your base leg.

- ✓ This one is all about opening the kua- the V of the hips- to give more room for internal movement.
- ✓ Gently push your lifted knee back and your hips forward.
- ✓ Maintain a straight line from your head to your base foot.
- ✓ Do both sides.

g. Snake creeps stretch.

Spread your feet wide apart. Not so wide that you can't still have the bottom of your feet on the floor.

Bend one knee and keep the other straight. This is designed to stretch the groin of the straight leg.

- ✓ Put your mind on the bottom of your feet.
- ✓ Point both hands to the foot of the straight leg.
- ✓ Squat down as deep or shallow as you want, but keep your feet on the floor.
- ✓ Swing your arms around like you are playing air guitar when you change sides. It makes the exercise more awesome.

2. Part two: Component training.

One of the ways that I like to divide things up so they make sense is to think about training a) Wei Jing, b) Nei Jing, c) Nei Chi, then d) Wei Chi. In Engrish, I mean English, that would be a) External Physical (Bone/Ligament/Tendon), b) Internal Physical (core, spine, earth), c) Internal Chi (moving chi with heaven and earth power), and d) External Chi (using your mind to make the chi bigger than your body, i.e. the waterfall and tsunami visualization thingy).

This section is about how to train the part "b" stuff, the internal physical. A lot of times, internal power masters will have students touch their belly so you can feel things moving around in there. This is not some mystical feat of incredible awesomeness. It is just a demonstration of deep core intelligent movement and agility.

Let's get to work on these so you can impress your friends with the amazing ability to wiggle your deep core as well! Oh, and this is good for massaging your organs and keeping them in the right shape and place as well- but who cares about all that "incredible health and well-being until you die as an ornery old person" stuff! Let's party!

a. Core agilities.

Stand still. Begin with trying to shrink and expand your core. The idea is to open and close it like an accordion. Make your hips go down and your ribs go up, but do it by moving your lower pelvic muscles down and your diaphragm up. Then relax. Then repeat. At first this will be difficult as you might not be very good at consciously using these muscle groups, but you can do it. Practice.

Next, play circles. Try to move a circle from the belly button, down to the perineum, around to the mingmen (lower back), and then back to the belly button. Use your mind to do this and try to get the muscles to move around to follow the pattern. Do this a few times and then reverse the circle.

After that, play figure eights. This is really kind of like doing two circles at once. Start with a vertical figure eight. Have one circle rotating down (the bottom circle of your figure eight), and the other circle rotating up (the top circle of your figure eight). The big idea is to add in shrinking and expanding to your core circle exercises.

Now add in different directions to the figure eights. Play a horizontal figure eight, play diagonal figure eights, play any direction you want!

We are trying to build core movement, aliveness, and intelligence- so there is no wrong way to move the core around. The only thing we want to avoid is locking muscles down so they cannot move. We are training movement and aliveness.

> **Chang San-Feng**
>
> The *ch'i* [vital life energy] should be excited,
>
> The *shen* [spirit of vitality] should be internally gathered.

b. Spinal expansion.

Stand with your feet shoulder width apart. Make sure your hair looks great. Now, relax. Melt your body. Start with your shoulders, then your chest, then your core, then your legs. You'll hear some people tell you to "engage your core," hmm, meh. Make it alive, and useful, but not tense and locked. Relax.

When we do core agilities we want the core to move around. Now we want it to be a relaxed volume. They call this "sinking the chi in the waist" in the Tai chi classics. Remember how a few minutes ago we worked on lifting the diaphragm up and down to build core intelligence? Yeah about that. Don't do that anymore. Let it sink.

Now sink the entire core, diaphragm down, lower pelvic muscles down, core relaxed down. At the same time lift the back of your head. Sink the mingmen (lower back) and lift the jade pillow (back of the head). Now work this action like a pump- separate them and then relax. Separate them and then relax. Core down and head up, then relax. You want your spine to feel alive like a snake.

c. Play the earth.

This exercise is kind of like almost jumping. Bend your knees a little bit, press into the floor like you are going to jump, but don't jump. Instead, play with the threshold of where the power of driving into the floor would lift you off of the ground but doesn't. Then take the force generated and send it up your spine.

This may read like bouncing with your feet not leaving the floor, but it isn't. Rather, you are attempting to play with the force generated by interacting with the earth without losing your sinking and melting. This means that you don't want to bounce up and down; keep your core sunk down while your feet play the earth.

Another thing I like to do is to play my feet like a cat kneading on your lap. You can also attach your hand to this motion: as your feet give pressure into the earth your hands are forced up like a leaping cat, and as your feet suck from the earth your hands go down. At first you may want to do this barefoot, but once you get the hang of it you can have any footwear you would like.

You can also play this while walking around. Same thing, you just move around.

d. Put it together.

Now do all of them at the same time! Sink your core, play the earth, and lift the head. Everything shrinking and expanding, opening and closing, separating and relaxing.

The core and the head separate. The core gives downward pressure to the feet. The feet press into the earth giving the head upward force.

Remember, this is internal physical, not chi stuff yet. Therefore you should actually, physically be moving stuff. Remember the old saying, *doing too much is the same as doing too little.* Don't try to break anything off of yourself by working this too hard, work it gently.

But, speaking of chi stuff...

3. Part three: Chi exercises.

Now it is time to practice that chi stuff. Begin by trying to make your body feel empty. Find your ghost inside of your physical body. Next, have the chi go down the front of your body to the ground and up the back. Start small. At first it can be a gentle stream of water that you visualize moving, and then you can increase the volume as you can visualize it. Chi goes down the front, displaces the earth chi, goes up your back, over your head, and down the front again.

Work on moving the chi around. Don't let it stay in one place. In that regard it will behave like water. If it moves it stays fresh and clears bad stuff away. If it stays in one place for too long it stagnates.

There are numerous chi building exercises you can do. You can focus on moving chi around

- ✓ inside of your body.
- ✓ On the surface of your body.
- ✓ In your bones.
- ✓ Outside of your body, in as large a volume as you can muster.
- ✓ Around the room.

- ✓ Around the area as far as you can see.
- ✓ Around the area as far as you can imagine!

How do you do all of this? With your Yi (mind, intention, awareness) of course. Get good at moving your mind around. Give it volume, shrinking and expanding, spiraling, yin and yang- you name it! Play as many games as you can moving chi around. After you are finished just put your mind back into the earth so chi doesn't stagnate anywhere. Easy peasy!

Let's go over some of the ways to wave your hands around while you play chi. To be honest, it doesn't really matter what kind of movements you choose as you are really trying to train your mind to move chi and chi to move your body. Here are some of the ones I like to do- but this is by no means whatsoever an exhaustive list.

a. Wave Hands.

Stand with your feet shoulder with apart. Lift your arms up in front of your body. Bring them back down again. Repeat as often as you feel like doing it.

- ✓ Remember- chi goes down as the arms go up.
- ✓ Earth chi goes up the back.
- ✓ Yin Yang Power. Opposing force power.
- ✓ Arms, shoulders and neck stay empty.
- ✓ Relax buddy.

b. Dancing bear.

Stand with your feet shoulder width apart. Use the bottom of your feet to spiral and rotate your body back and forth.

- ✓ Head up, neck empty.
- ✓ Think about your chi body, not your physical body.
- ✓ Let your arms relax, but don't try to fly away. Keep chi going through them so they don't turn to jelly.

c. **Big circles, or "the double ninja chop."**

Step out into a wider stance. Bring your hands in and up in the middle of your body, and then out and down in big circles to the sides of your body. You want to make two big circles that form a sideways eight.

Like a ninja chopping down on a bad guy to your right and to your left at the same time. You are that awesome.

- ✓ Use your chi body.
- ✓ Do not let your arms extend past your chi body.
- ✓ Do not disconnect your arms from the feet and earth reaction force.
- ✓ Work shrinking and expanding, chi counterweighting, earth power.

d. Touch the sky.

Stand in a wide stance just like with the big ninja double chop thing. Bring your hands in front of your belly. Push them up over your head so you look like a giant star fish. Bring them back down on the same path.

This is a great exercise for working heaven and earth power.

✓ Head up, chi goes down.
✓ Chi goes from the hands into your

body, even if the arms physically are going away from your body.
- ✓ Shoulders down, especially if your arms are going up.
- ✓ Train the chi body, not the physical.

Remember to always work on distinguishing the physical body from the chi body, and the chi body from the spirit body. The absolute key to getting to a reasonably high level with this practice is to distinguish the three different bodies that you have and then figure out how to make them interact.

The mind leads the chi and the chi leads the body. This is a key truth and practice for you to work and live by!

e. Scoop the moon on three sides.

Stand with your feet shoulder width apart. Bring your hands over your head. Use your feet to spiral your body to the right. Squat down a little bit and scoop your arms on the right side like you are picking something up from the ground. Then do the same thing to the left, and then the facing straight ahead.

- ✓ As always, chi goes down as the hands go up.
- ✓ Use the feet to spiral, not the waist!
- ✓ In reality you are not scooping chi from the earth, you are giving chi to the earth and accepting chi back. Do not try to take the earth chi, that won't do you any good.

f. Play the ball.

Stand with your feet slightly more than shoulder width apart. Pretend that you are holding a beach ball big enough to go from chest to fingertips. Then roll your arms around like you are turning the ball around inside of your grasp.

- ✓ Use your feet to create spiraling for the side to side aspect of the motion.
- ✓ Use counterweight power and earth reaction force to make your arms go up and down.
- ✓ Keep your back rounded and chest sucked in to create the circle.
- ✓ Play chi body.

g. Splitting, or "the human tornado."

Stand with your feet wide apart. Bring your hands together, one on top of the other, in front of your body. Now make one hand go out to the side in a downward arc and the other go to the other side in an upward arc.

Then bring them back together again in front of your body.

- ✓ Play your feet.
- ✓ Do not let your hands get outside of the connection to your chi body.
- ✓ Chi goes down, earth power, and so on.

h. End with Standing Pole.

Stand there with your feet shoulder width apart and your hands raised out in front of you like you are holding beach ball. Let your whole body relax down, chi down, and your spirit is up. When I was first learning internal martial arts I was told to do this for at least 20 minutes a day. I recommend that you not worry about time at all, just stand this way as long as you feel like doing it. Remember, it is a standing meditation.

To close at the end of your workout bring your hands up in big circles at the sides of your body and bring them back down to just over your belly button. And you're done!

This whole thing should take about 15 or so minutes.

As I wrap this book up, here are some things to consider!

Practice, practice, practice! Just remember to be patient with yourself, don't give up on yourself, and enjoy the ride. An Internal Power practice is about finding the deeper layers of yourself, feeling better about yourself, and becoming more of what you are capable of becoming.

The more you do this over time the more refined and better it will get. The difference between a master of internal power and a novice is only time and practice.

Be willing to have a flexible mind as you train. In many cases the key to personal improvement is to be willing to change your paradigm and world view. The only thing that can ever hold you back from personal growth is you.

Also, I do strongly recommend that you pursue finding a qualified teacher. You can attend seminars, workshops, or classes- whatever you can get your hands on.

Use this book as a sounding board for what you hear elsewhere. I'm not going to say that I know everything with perfect perfection, but I do know quite a bit on this subject. This book is a very good guide and gives you some very solid ideas on what to look for. Make sure that your teacher is actually in the game and not just wasting your time doing forms or whatever without any true internal power practice.

Shameless plug! This book is only the beginning of internal power information that I have to share. Stick around and look for more books, videos and other stuff to come!

Extra stuff and other thoughts.

Kinetic Testing

George Xu testing Otmar Olsina in my school in Asheville, NC 2012.

Kinetic testing is how you can tell if you are doing this stuff right or not. It relies on something called Ting Jing, which translates to "listening power." A lot of times Jing translates to "power." But don't think of it as a super power or magic or anything like that. A better translation would be "acquired skill."

Listening skill is the ability to touch somebody and feel what's going on inside of their body. By touching you anywhere on your body, a person accomplished in this skill set can tell where your structure is wrong, where you don't have chi going through, if you do or do not have internal power, earth power, etc. All with a touch. I do this all of the time.

I call this kinetic testing because you can touch somebody and feel if their movement is on the right track or not.

There are four basic levels to this. The great thing about these tests is that both people involved are practicing. One is practicing listening, and the other is practicing body quality. Win/ win situations are awesome. Make sure to communicate with each other as you do these tests. Talk about what you feel that is right and what needs work. If you are doing the body quality part talk to the listening partner about how much pressure they are giving (too much, too little?) for you to practice with.

Level 1: Standing. Have the person you are testing just stand there. Gently apply pressure to their forehead, then chest, then belly. See if you feel chi going through, any breaks in the body, earth reaction force, etc. Look for everything you have read about in this book.

Next stand behind the person and push straight down on their shoulders. Again, you should feel no breaks. This one is especially good for testing the hips alignment.

You can push anywhere on the person's body to see if their power is consistent.

Level 2: Static Posture. Pick a static posture with your hands up. It doesn't matter which one, but generally you would try to cover the six directions with your arms: arms out front, arms to the sides, arms up, arms back, arms down but not touching your body. Do the exact same thing to test as in level 1, give gentle steady pressure to whatever you are trying to test to look for qualities and mistakes. Also, test all six directions on the person's arms for each posture: press down, up, in, out, forward, and backward.

Level 3: Moving the arms. This time stand in the same place, but have the person being tested move their arms, again trying to cover all six directions. A good way to think about it this time is to have circles instead of lines. Think of having a circle that goes horizontal, then one that goes vertically from front to back, and a third that goes vertically from side to side. Move the arms in variations of these circles.

I recommend that you begin with just bringing the hands up and down in front of the body. Then you can test other directions of up and down and so on.

Level 4: Moving the feet. Now can you do the exact same tests, but while walking around? If you can only root or only move, your skill is not as valuable as if you can root and move around freely and lightly at the same time. They call this being light but heavy. If you think this cannot be done you need to study animal movement more. Watch a tiger walk around- they are light on their feet, but heavy. Try pushing one over to see what happens.

This ability is to have a root but no root. It is important because we want to be able to apply the internal power qualities mentioned in this book all of the time, moving or still. Only then are they most valuable.

What if you don't have somebody to test you? Well then you don't. You'll have to go to events, workshops, seminars, classes, and catch as catch can.

What if (and I've had this problem over the years) you have a friend or significant other that you ask to help you, but they are not very cooperative and generally just push you over too fast while you are still trying to get it right? I recommend that you communicate the fact before you get them to touch you that they need to go slow because you don't have it right yet and need their help to practice.

Though it isn't as good, you can also test yourself in an isometric format. Have one arm push on the other in some fashion to see if you can create the correct quality. I do this all of the time.

Kinetic testing really is the only way to know if you are on the right track. Any internal power practice must have testing in some fashion or another just so you know if you are even close to correct. I've met people who have taken part in internal power practices for decades but never did any testing. They tend to be very disheartened when then discover the serious mistakes they've been making!

Therefore, you need to find a way to do some testing. You may wish to check out the events by me or my teacher George Xu. Also, any WACIMA (Worldwide Association of Chinese Internal Martial Arts) certified instructor can help you with this.

Sucking Power

One of the things to work on is your ability to suck. Yeah, I know, this doesn't sound so good. It sounds like when a Chinese master teaches you to work on "third leg power", or when they try to teach you the technique of "Golden Cock stand on one leg."

Sucking power means that you suck your arms and your diaphragm in. Suck the diaphragm into the mingmen (lower back). It means that you have the yin chi in front of you come in to expand with the yang chi behind you.

It means that you consume the power of your opponent and allow it to go through you to add to the power behind you. It means that you are empty and take on nothing yourself, so when you are given force, that force attacks nothing- you don't care.

The Predator Theory

Move your body like a predatory animal. I don't mean that you should go on a killing spree, I mean that you should look at characteristics of how certain animals move.

A predatory animal is light, but heavy when it walks. Watch a wolf trot around. Watch a tiger walk. They are relaxed and nimble, yet still very powerful looking.

A predatory animal is still, but alive. A lioness can sit in the tall grass completely still and relaxed, but with such an aliveness and mental alertness that it can move explosively at any time.

A predatory animal can move explosively, but with a relaxed intensity. You will never see a tiger flexing every muscle in its body and stiffen up to move. Yet you will also never see one so relaxed that it does not respond to what is around it.

Have your feet control your hands.

To do animal style internal arts you do not pretend to be an animal, you do not imitate an animal, you become that animal spiritually.

George Xu

"He who has no technique will defeat he who has technique. To see the emptiness creates the technique, like the tiger that chases the rabbit. The tiger doesn't have a chasing technique but all the techniques are melted inside of the tiger. When the tiger attacks it "sees" the technique in that moment. This defeats the mind limited on technique, on jin (physical strength), on qi (internal power), on yi (mind), or to be focused on something."

Practice, not Philosophy

I can always tell when somebody isn't getting what I am trying to communicate to them when they tell me that I am discussing philosophy. No. I am teaching you a series of practices. It's not the same thing.

A practice is something that you do with your mind and your body. A philosophy is something that you pontificate about.

You can never learn to actually do something if you just sit around, talk about it, and never actually take the first step.

In this regard, never trust a skinny chef and never trust an overweight martial arts or fitness consultant.

Another thought along these same lines is developing the skills to determine at what level a practitioner is working. Of course, the best way is to shake their hand and read their quality, but failing that look for key words in their conversation. Build your powers of assessment.

Do they talk about techniques and movements? Low level physical.

Do they talk about physical things to do with the body? Physical (jing).

Do they talk about core (dan tien)? Internal physical.

Do they talk about chi as it moves through the body? Listen more to see if they are confused about where the physical ends and the chi begins. Most people in internal martial arts are here somewhere.

Do they talk about chi body as a separate body- mind leads chi, and chi leads body? Chi body.

Do they talk about chi, but it's kind of airy fairy sounding? Low level, they don't really understand what they are talking about. "Move the chi around like a beautiful pristine river of gorgeous butterflies floating up to the sky and be in love." Gag.

Do they talk about emptiness, mind body, and spirit power? Probably pretty high level. When you touch this person you should feel strong empty power that seems to come from nowhere. Listen to this person.

Remember, look at these as assessments, not judgments. A person is where they are. I have one kid in second grade and another in college right now. I love them both, they are just in different places in their education. The same concept applies here as well. But it does do you a lot of good to be able to tell the difference.

George Xu

Wu Wei (no effort) defeats You Wei (have effort). Not having a Fist defeats having a Fist. Not having a Root defeats having a Root. Not having a technique defeats having a technique.

What to look for in a video.

I am a big advocate of watching videos on youtube.com or any other site to look for body quality and internal power. You should as well, and do not discriminate what activity the person in question in doing. Watch whatever activity you are interested in watching. I, of course, watch mostly martial art videos- but it doesn't have to be. We are studying optimal human potential- so who cares what the person is trying to optimize.

Here are a few tips on how to assess internal power body quality from video.

- ✓ For martial arts videos, viewers tend to discriminate based on race. Obviously an oriental person saying he is a master must be good right? Wrong. A lot of them suck. A lot of them are great. You have to watch with a non-racist eye.
- ✓ If you watch a video and are not sure, read the comments. As a rule of thumb, if the comments think it is awesome there is a good chance it's low level. Real high level internal power shouldn't look real because all of the movement is hidden inside.

- ✓ If you think something might be high level, watch the behavior of the person being thrown. Well, if there is one. Does this person look like he is being thrown by an external force, or does he look like he is bouncing away under his own power? Does he look like he is playing along too much and hamming it up too much?
- ✓ If there is no person being thrown, or he looks like he is in fact actually being thrown, look at the star of the video. Does he or she look melted and relaxed, yet seem light and empty? Is there total body unity? Think about all of the things you read about in this book and try to identify them in a checklist.
- ✓ You get better with practice. Assess, don't judge.
- ✓ Do not comment on the video unless you are making positive comments. Do not try to correct the person. Remember, it takes courage to post something. Don't be a troll.

Some masters to look up to see good quality are George Xu, Ma Hong, Chen Xiaowang, and Wu Ji. Not an exhaustive list of course, but a starting point.

The Internal Power Cheat Sheet.

It is said that "the spirit is the leader and the body follows its command". If you can lift your spirit, then your movements will naturally be agile and alive.

The Correct Body, by Yang Cheng Fu.

1. Relax the neck and suspend the head.
2. Sink the Chest and Raise the Back.
3. Relax the Waist, sink the chi.
4. Distinguish Solid and Empty.
5. Sink the Shoulders and Elbows.
6. Use the Mind and not Brute Force.
7. Coordinate your Upper and Lower Body.
8. Unify your Internal and External.
9. Continuity - No Stopping.
10. Seek Serenity in Activity.

When Tai Chi is in motion, the positive and the negative separate: when Tai Chi stops, the positive and the negative integrate.

Concepts to keep in mind.

1. The Mind (Yi) Leads the Chi, and the Chi Leads to Body (Jing).

2. Distinguish the physical body from the chi body, yin from yang.

3. Keep your body loose, open, empty, and sunk.

4. Internal power should sink to the lower part of the abdomen. Raise your spirit.

5. Doing too much is the same as doing too little.

6. Stand like a perfectly balanced scale and move like a turning wheel. Do not be double weighted.

7. The opponent does not know me; I alone know him.

8. Yin and yang mutually aid and change each other.

> After coming to an understanding of the internal power of movement, you can approach the theory of natural awareness.

Made in the USA
Middletown, DE
12 August 2015